nourish

nourish

AMBER LOCKE

vibrant salads to relish & refresh

MITCHELL BEAZLEY

An Hachette UK Company
www.hachette.co.uk

First published in Great Britain in 2016
by Mitchell Beazley, a division of
Octopus Publishing Group Ltd
Carmelite House
50 Victoria Embankment
London EC4Y 0DZ
www.octopusbooks.co.uk

ISBN 978-1-78472-178-7

A CIP catalogue record for this book is available
from the British Library.

Printed and bound in Italy

10 9 8 7 6 5 4 3 2 1

Publishing Director Stephanie Jackson
Art Director & Designer Yasia Williams-Leedham
Editor Pollyanna Poulter
Copy Editor Nicola Graimes
Nutritionist Angela Dowden
Assistant Production Manager Caroline Alberti
Photographer Amber Locke

CONTENTS

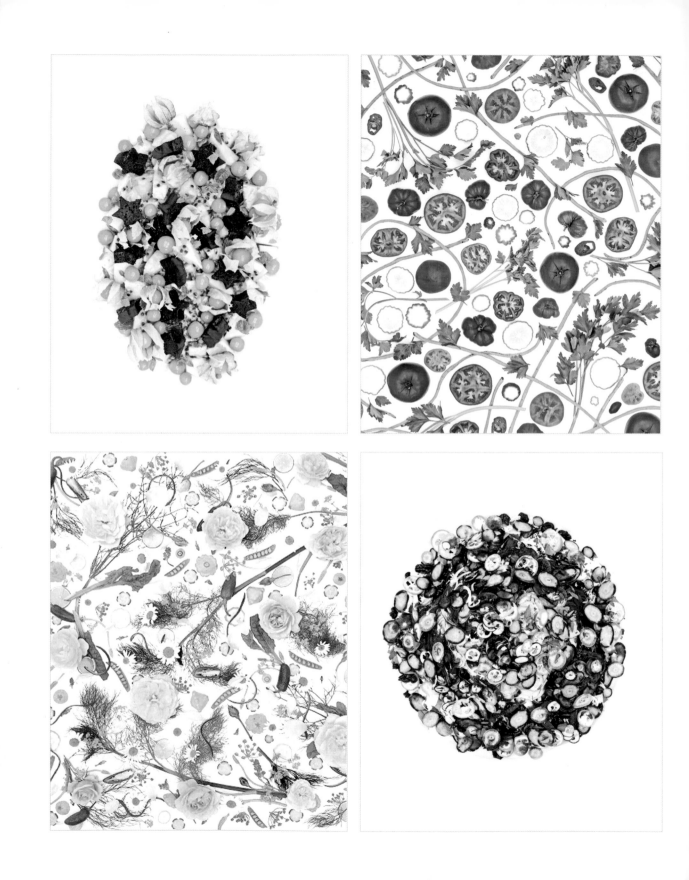

introduction

ABOUT ME

I come from a family of passionate foodies and was fortunate to grow up with enthusiastic gardeners as parents so we always had a large vegetable plot and a bountiful supply of fruit, vegetables, salad crops and herbs. My mother is a talented cook and bought me up to appreciate good ingredients and with an ingrained desire to create beautiful, nourishing food – a meal had to contain at least seven different colours for it to constitute a proper healthy meal! Unsurprisingly, salads at home were lovingly made, super-colourful seasonal delights, and this was the start of my passion for fresh fruit and veg and healthy food in general.

MY LOVE OF RAW FOOD

People choose to eat a raw food diet for all sorts of reasons but for me it was purely curiosity. I'd stumbled across the concept while reading an article in *Vogue* magazine and was really intrigued by the idea. After some research I decided to try it out for a few weeks... and wow! I was absolutely blown away with how incredible it made me feel – I had a crazy amount of energy, distinctly improved mental clarity, a wonderful feeling of well being, and I slept incredibly well too. Two years down the line, I now eat about 80–90 per cent raw food, depending on the season, and I find this way of eating works really well for me.

I appreciate raw food might sound a bit outlandish, not particularly appetizing or hard work, but it can be so tasty and rewarding. So if you're intrigued to try it for yourself, I recommend starting with just one raw meal a day, either a breakfast smoothie or a big raw salad for lunch or dinner. Build it up from there, and see how you feel.

When I started eating raw food it gave me a new appreciation of fresh fruit and vegetables and a fascination for creating ever-more flavourful and eye-catching salads. And after more than two years of daily salad-making, I'm still super-enthusiastic about them. For me, it's a treat at the end of the day to spend a little time in the kitchen and find different ways of creating big bowls of goodness that are not only satisfying for me and my family's appetite (we love food and like to eat a lot!), but that also taste amazing.

I love discovering new ingredients, finding new ways of preparing fruit and veg and playing around with flavour and taste combinations. I'm always amazed at the infinite variety and beauty of natural ingredients, which is why I started to create designs with them.

I also get great pleasure from growing some of my own produce and I gravitate to the more unusual heritage and heirloom varieties as they have such diversity in colour, taste, shape and texture. Even if it's just picking a few fresh herbs from the garden, there's a real sense of achievement using an ingredient you've grown yourself.

ABOUT THIS BOOK

Raw salads play a major part of most raw diets, but don't think of them as just summer food or a light, unsatisfying meal made up of a few sparse, soul-less lettuce leaves. Salads can be big, bold, delicious, nutritious and satisfying. Then there are the knock-your-socks-off dressings and toppings that will raise your bowl of wonderfulness to a whole other dimension.

This book encapsulates what I love about raw food, and salads in particular. Alongside the recipes for both sweet and savoury salads, all styled and photographed by myself, you'll find a chapter on dressings and toppings as well as tips on ingredients, cutting styles and techniques. Each salad recipe comes with an explanation of its key nutrients and health benefits as well as ideas of how to adapt it to appeal to different tastes, diets and eating occasions. So you'll find ideas for cooked additions and non-vegan and non-vegetarian variations scattered throughout the recipes.

Each salad recipe serves 2–4 people but as a raw fruit- and veg-based diet is one of abundance, the portion sizes are typically on the large size, so please adjust the quantities to suit your appetite and nutritional requirements.

I really hope you enjoy reading this book as much as I did creating it, and that you find my recipes and photographs both visually and gastronomically interesting.

Viva la veg!

Amber

WHAT MAKES A GOOD SALAD?

A salad can be as simple or as complex as you wish, and more elaborate preparation is by no means always better. A plate of thickly sliced sun-ripened tomatoes need nothing more than a sprinkle of sea salt, a glug of good cold-pressed extra virgin olive oil and a scattering of basil leaves to enhance their natural perfection. For me, sometimes just a bowl of grated carrot with a basic vinaigrette hits the ultimate gustatory spot, particularly when I'm short of time.

I personally eat a HUGE salad at least once a day. More often than not I'll make it out of whatever I have to hand in the fridge, on the counter top, in the greenhouse or in the garden. Sometimes I'll plan and shop specially and enjoy a longer and almost meditative process of chopping, grating and slicing to create a more elaborate dish. You can even eat salad for breakfast as a blended green smoothie or juice.

People often baulk at eating salads in the colder months but if you add rich and spicy dressings (flavoured with ginger, garlic and spices, for example), include carb-dense vegetables, such as carrots, sweet potatoes and celeriac, and throw in extra nuts and seeds, then you instantly have a more satisfying and 'warming' salad. If you're a non-raw eater then the addition of cooked veg, warm dressings or sauces and hot toppings will definitely do the trick.

We sometimes think of salads being predominantly savoury in flavour but adding fruits, such as strawberries, blueberries and figs, to your vegetable creations all work brilliantly. They also look lovely and give a pleasant soft texture and sweetness to your final dish.

It's always worth remembering that we eat first with the eyes, so it pays to make an effort with presentation, using good-quality fresh ingredients and incorporating a range of colours and textures.

The best way to start a salad is with fresh, preferably seasonal and organic produce for both flavour and health. If only buying organic produce, try to choose ones from the Clean 15 list and avoid the Dirty 'Dozen' (see opposite). The principle being that thick-skinned fruit and veg absorb less pesticides than thin-skinned fruit and veg.

THE DIRTY 'DOZEN' & CLEAN 15

Since this list first originated in 2013 kale, collard greens and peppers have made it to the Dirty Dozen list making it a Dirty 14 instead*. Although this list is frequently quoted, one should bear in mind that it is American in origin and the types of chemicals and the levels of pesticides used may differ from those in other parts of the world, although the principles remain the same.

*See the EWG Shopper's Guide to Pesticides in Produce report, www.ewg.org

DIRTY 'DOZEN'
1. apples 2. peaches 3. nectarines 4. strawberries 5. grapes 6. celery 7. spinach
8. peppers 9. cucumbers 10. cherry tomatoes 11. snap/sugar peas 12. potatoes
13. chilli peppers 14. kale/collard greens

CLEAN 15
1. avocados 2. sweetcorn 3. pineapples 4. cabbage 5. peas (frozen) 6. onions
7. asparagus 8. mangoes 9. papayas 10. kiwi 11. aubergine 12. grapefruit
13. canteloupe melon 14. cauliflower 15. sweet potatoes

TOP TIPS FOR THE BEST SALADS

1. Choose a variety of fresh produce for nutritional value as well as for taste, colour, texture and aesthetics.

2. Buy the freshest, good-quality produce you can. See 'Tips & Tricks' on page 17 for the best ways to wash and store your salad ingredients for maximum freshness and longevity.

3. Make sure your ingredients are dry. This is so important, especially with delicate salad leaves, as a dressing won't coat a wet leaf and you want to avoid a soggy salad.

4. Try to ensure each forkful contains different elements, such as salad leaves, vegetables, fresh herbs, crunchy bits, chewy bits, juicy bits and a hint of sweetness (from fruit or from the dressing) to give a balance of flavours and textures.

5. Some salads with more delicate leaves are best with a fresh, light dressing, whereas others with more robust leaves and ingredients can stand up to stronger-tasting, heavier, rich or creamy dressings.

6. If you're serving your salad dressed, then add it little by little to avoid it being swamped and turning soggy. Unless it's a slaw that benefits from pre-dressing, choose to dress your salad at the last minute (see pages 122–4).

7. Add some extra 'kerb appeal' with a few finishing touches (see toppings pages 136–140).

FLAVOUR GRID

Ingredients can be grouped according to base flavour profiles. Using a balanced selection of these with a suitable dressing will result in interesting, well-flavoured salads. As a general guide:

Neutral: most soft-leaf lettuce, cabbage, bok choy, spinach, avocado, mushrooms, cucumber

Grassy: celery, asparagus, swiss chard, fennel, green beans, herbs

Spicy: watercress, rocket, radishes, horseradish, turnip, chillies, garlic, onions, leeks, ginger, basil, mustard cress, mustard greens

Sweet: fennel, peppers, carrots, beetroot, peas, sweetcorn, sweet potato, parsnip, (ripe) tomatoes, fresh fruit and berries

Sour: citrus fruit, rhubarb, green papaya, sorrel, (less-ripe) tomatoes, lemon grass

Bitter: endive, chicory, bitter melon, kale, okra, dandelion leaves, aubergine, radicchio, puntarelle, broccoli

Neutral

Bitter

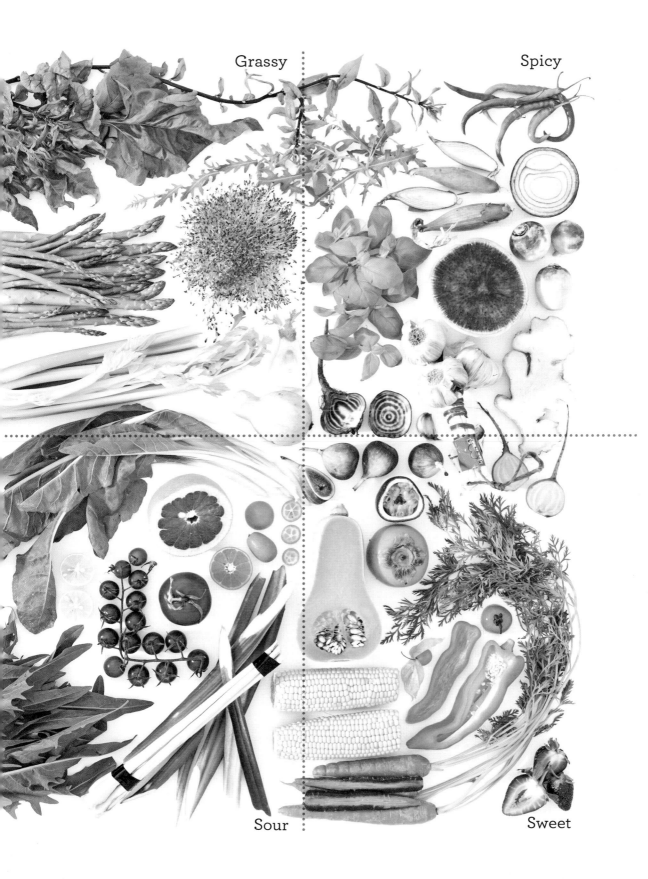

Grassy

Spicy

Sour

Sweet

SALAD STYLE

If I'm making a salad for just myself I tend to gravitate towards the same favourite bowl time and time again but if I'm feeding several people I love to present them on large decorative platters, as it spreads out the ingredients and there's more room to make them look attractive.

Any food looks more appealing served in a pretty bowl or on a platter. I mainly use white crockery (and occasionally black or slate grey) as I like the colours of the ingredients to really pop and stand out. I also sometimes layer a salad like a trifle in a straight-sided glass bowl. If I'm taking a salad to work or on a picnic I use a big screw-top glass jar and add the ingredients in layers as I cut them up.

Salads can be presented in all sorts of ways and you can really have some fun. They can be laid out like a mandala, arranged in a chequerboard pattern, or just chop all the ingredients up, chuck them together in a big bowl and mix them up with your hands.

SALAD PREP

I love the challenge of coming back from a farmers' market or supermarket shop and deciding exactly what to do with the produce I've bought. So in preparation of my 'prep', I usually lay out the fresh produce on my kitchen table and mentally run through all the things I could do with each one and how the ingredients may work together. The variety of preparation permutations are endless (a 'hundred and one ways with a carrot' anyone?) and even the most basic lettuce leaves can be chopped, torn into bite-sized pieces, shredded, grilled, braised or used as an alternative for tacos or wraps. The challenge of making something creative and inspired with the most basic fruit and veg is what I sometimes have the most fun with. While there are lots of suggestions and ideas in this book, I encourage you to experiment with your own raw style.

A bed of raw vegetables and/or green leaves is always my favourite way to start making a salad and these things make the super-healthy base of all the salads I eat. I then add in a selection of other 'savoury' fruit and veg, then maybe a few sweet or tart elements to add little bursts of flavour and finally a sprinkle of super-food ingredients or garnishes. Sometimes I add a few cooked veg or some carbs or proteins but greens and raw vegetables always

make up the majority percentage, with other elements just supplementing or adding (complementary or contrasting) flavours, textures, decorations or extra nutritional hits to super-charge my salad bowl!

There are some vegetables, especially root vegetables, that you possibly wouldn't instantly think of eating raw, such as sweet potatoes, Jerusalem artichokes, cauliflower, broccoli stems, butternut squash, celeriac, turnip. But, sliced very thinly, they can be incredibly palatable and nutritious. If you buy your carrots and beets organic don't hesitate to use the carrot tops and beetroot leaves and stems as they are delicious and pack an amazing nutritional punch.

The following lists contain some pointers to the types of fresh ingredients I often use when making salads, to help you on your salad journey:

GREENS, SUCH AS:

❋ **Lettuce:** baby gem, butterhead, iceberg (often derided as bland and watery but when chilled and cut finely gives a great cool crunch to a salad), romaine, cos, frisée, oak leaf, rocket, bok choy, Chinese leaves, lambs lettuce

❋ **Radicchio:** chicory/endive, castlefranco, frisée

❋ **Dark leafy greens:** spinach, watercress, kale, Swiss chard, dandelion leaves (these are all super good for you – the darker the green colour the better!)

❋ **Cabbage family greens:** kale, Savoy cabbage, Brussels sprouts

❋ **Samphire, seaweed** or other edible sea vegetables

❋ **Sprouting seeds and beans:** sunflower sprouts

❋ **Micro greens:** baby kale, pea shoots, micro herbs

❋ **Beetoot leaves and carrot tops**

❋ **Handfuls of fresh chopped herbs**

❋ **Other lower nutrient-dense greens:** broccoli, fennel, cucumber, celery, courgettes, green beans, snow peas, sugar snap peas, broad beans

'SAVOURY' RAW FRUIT & VEG, SUCH AS:

❋ radishes, celery, asparagus, kohlrabi, cauliflower, onion/ spring onions, wild garlic, mushrooms, avocado, cabbage, artichoke, okra, mooli

'SWEET' RAW FRUIT & VEG, SUCH AS:

❋ peppers, sweetcorn, tomatoes, carrots, sweet potato, butternut squash

❋ apples, papaya, peaches, apricots, grapes, figs, kiwi, clementine, pineapple, blueberries, strawberries, raspberries

❋ dried fruits, such as sultanas, raisins, dates, figs

INGREDIENT SPECIFICS

ONIONS It's often nice to add an 'onion-y' element to a salad as it gives it an instant savouriness and with its strong flavour, makes it seem more satisfying. Finely chopped spring onions are great, as are chives and shallots which have a much milder flavour than white onions. Red onions are sweeter and cooked onions (roasted, braised, barbecued or caramelized) are a really nice addition, too. It's also worth giving larger onions (red or white or even shallots sometimes) a quick pickle before you use them. This will cut the acidity, making them milder (and more palatable to onion-haters).

I always chop onions into super-super fine micro dice or tracing paper thin slices using my mandolin as, unless you're a raw onion lover, getting a big chunk of raw onion can be an unpleasant experience and overpower other flavours in the salad. Alternatively, a shake of onion salt or spoonful of onion chutney in a salad dressing is another way of working in this flavour.

GARLIC If you'd like a hint of garlic in your salad then rub a cut clove of garlic lightly round the inside of your salad bowl and it will delicately flavour your salad as you mix it. Alternatively, put a peeled clove in a jar of dressing for 30 minutes and fish it out before you serve your salad. It will give a gentle flavouring to your dressing.

CAULIFLOWER has become a super-trendy veg due to its versatility. Roasted it takes on new flavours, while cooked and mashed it works as a low-carb replacement for traditional mashed potatoes. By baking into a crust you can make low-carb/gluten-free pizza bases. Very finely chopped or grated it takes on a plausible grain-like texture and perfect rice replacement. Mixed into salads it gives a pleasing texture and sucks up a dressing really well.

FIBROUS VEGETABLES that you might usually cook (like beetroot or squash) can be grated or sliced super-finely to make them easier to digest. Sometimes it's worth marinating them or just dressing and setting aside for a while to soften – this works really well with things like coleslaw as the fibres of the cabbage soften so they're easier to chew. Don't overlook Jerusalem artichokes, which are really great raw. Peeled and finely sliced or grated, they add a sweet crispy crunch similar to Chinese water chestnut.

CHARRED corn, roasted peppers, courgettes, mushrooms, squash and aubergine are great non-raw salad additions and give a wonderful smoky flavour. Grill halves of citrus fruit before squeezing their juice into a dressing for a beyond delicious flavour. Next time you have your barbecue out it's worth cooking a few extra things to bung in your salads during the week – it's amazing how grateful you can be for a few pre-roasted veg, especially with a wonderful smoky aroma, when you come to make them.

PICKLES and fermented foods have a great sweet/sour tang. As well as being full of fantastic gut-friendly bacteria, they can really bump up the flavour – so grab a jar of kimchi or sauerkraut and add it to your next salad.

HERBS are a great way of adding a fresh taste and a flavour 'brightness' to salads. Mint (either chopped or whole leaves) works brilliantly in most salads. It's fun to use a spectrum of different herbs in your salads throughout the year. Dried herbs are great in dressings, too.

Commonly used herbs include: basil, thyme, parsley, oregano, marjoram, coriander and chives. It's certainly worth growing some of these if you can. It's also fun to try some more unusual herbs, such as lemon verbena or lemon balm (especially in salads with a fruit element), marjoram, sweet cecily, lovage, summer and winter savory, the Japanese herb 'shiso' or the sweet liquorice-tasting 'anise hyssop' (if you can get hold of some).

EDIBLE FLOWERS add visual interest, fragrance and sometimes a subtle floral taste. Ensure you're using blooms free from pesticides or preservatives (flowers from the florist or supermarket aren't a good idea) and that they are actually edible – check a reliable online resource if you're not sure.

Some of the floral, vegetable and herb flowers I like to use include: nasturtiums, marigolds, pansies, roses, sunflowers, daisies, fuchsias, lavender, courgette, radicchio, runner bean, broad bean, sage, chive, borage, thyme, fennel, bronze fennel, dill and purple basil.

NUTS AND SEEDS Although they are high in fat, nuts and seeds are a great addition to a salad as they add protein, fibre and a whole host of super-nutrients. You can use them plain, toast and roast them, coat them in spices or caramelize them. Leave them whole, or crumble, crush or grate them. It's sometimes even nice to crush some and grate others, so the small gritty bits coat the salad ingredients and give a pleasant additional texture.

SALT If you're trying to reduce the level of salt in your diet then it's great to use naturally salty-tasting ingredients in your salad or dressing. Some vegetables, such as tomatoes, bok choy, celery, samphire, beetroot and spinach, and herbs such as basil, have a naturally higher sodium level. Celery can be dried and ground into a great-tasting 'salt' alternative, as can the stems of Swiss chard. I often use the leaves of rainbow chard for the 'leafy' salad part and then very finely chop the stems so they look like confetti scattered over salads.

Left: Carrot roses take practice but prove just how stunning a plate of salad can be.
Right: Sweet & Sour Veggie 'Noodles' (see page 84).

WHY COOK SOME VEG?

Cooking some foods can decrease their nutritional value, for example water-soluble vitamins, such as vitamin C, can leach out into cooking water or be degraded by heat. However, some foods have a better nutritional value when cooked. For example, the levels of lycopene in cooked tomatoes is higher and more bioavailable than in raw tomatoes. Include an element of both cooked and raw food for a balanced diet.

Some other reasons to include cooked veg:

✳ cooked fruit and veg often taste significantly different than when raw, especially when using different cooking methods such as steaming, roasting, braising, baking or grilling.

✳ for variety and interest – they add a contrast of different flavours and textures to a meal

✳ some veg are easier to digest when cooked, especially more fibrous ones such as broccoli and green beans

✳ they add some warmth and an element of 'grounding' to a raw meal/salad (which can be especially welcome in the colder months) without the lethargic and slow-digesting heaviness that some cooked grains and pulses can give

✳ they add an element of quicker satisfaction/satiation but still keep a dish light and easily digested

Try these great cooked additions in your salad bowl:

✳ roasted or grilled veg: baby carrots, peppers, root veg, squash, radishes, cauliflower, leeks

✳ grilled lettuce or fennel, seared slices of cucumber, smoke steamed broccoli, caramelized Brussels sprouts, thick slices of steak-like seared portobello mushrooms

✳ steamed or sautéed green beans, sugar snaps, snow peas, bok choy, broccoli florets

✳ caramelized or grilled figs, peach, apple, pear, rhubarb

✳ elements from other cooked recipes, such as mini beetroot burgers, garlic mushrooms, ratatouille

✳ some vegetables are completely indigestible raw, such as white potatoes, and so have to be cooked to be edible

Also don't ignore the virtues of preserved, bottled and frozen veg that can give an instant flavour or texture boost to a salad. It's always worth having a few of these on standby just in case.

EXTRA PROTEIN OR CARBS?

To supplement your raw veg-based super-salad you can, of course, add in extra protein and/or carbs as your nutritional and dietary requirements and taste dictate.

✳ Proteins, such as nuts and seeds, tofu and tempeh, make great vegan-friendly options and faro, quinoa, bulgar wheat, freekeh, couscous, wholemeal and corn pasta, brown and wild rice, barley, rice noodles, beans, lentils, split peas, chickpeas, mung beans and forbidden rice (the type you can just soak and eat raw) are super, whole-food carb choices.

✳ Extra carbs are an easy way to bulk up a salad and especially important if you expend a lot of energy or do a lot of exercise. This type of ingredient always soaks up more dressing than vegetables so adjust your quantities of salad dressing accordingly.

✳ For omnivores it's also easy to add non-vegan protein options, such as cheese, eggs, fish or meat, to any of the salads in this book. This is an easy way to make one base salad cater for all.

SALAD TIPS & TRICKS

A few tips and tricks to help with your salad-crafting:

GO FOR VARIETY Eat the rainbow of colours of fruit and veg. Not only is it more interesting to vary what you buy and eat but you also get a lot more benefit from eating a wide range than the same ones (even super-food ones) all the time.

KEEP IT AS RAW AS POSSIBLE Eat some vegetables (most if possible) raw and try not to overcook the rest, as heat degrades the nutrients, especially water-soluble ones that are prone to leach into the water.

MAKE TIME Unless you're opting for a bowl of ready-prepared leaves or a bowl of simply chopped or grated veg it can certainly take time to make a more elaborate salad and an extra-special dressing. I save as much time as possible by preparing things the night before (for lunchtime salads), using the grating discs on my food processor, and always keep a jar of my basic vinaigrette dressing in the fridge so I have an immediate standby. However, when I have the time I look forward to the meditative-type ritual of washing, chopping, blending and mixing and cherish the opportunity to present my loved ones with a huge bowl of goodness prepared with love and care.

Left: Smashed Cucumber Salad (see page 74).

WASHING DELICATE LETTUCE AND HERBS If you have time to wash your produce before you store it then it's a great way to save time when you come round to preparing your salad. When your salad leaves are too delicate for a salad spinner, place them in a bowl or sink of cold water, agitate the leaves with both hands to wash off any dirt, let them sit for a few minutes to allow the dirt to settle to the bottom of the bowl, then use both hands with your fingers spread wide to fish the leaves out of the water and let as much water drain from them as possible. Place on a tea towel covered with absorbent kitchen paper then gently roll up or fold into a parcel, place in a plastic bag and put in the salad or crisper draw in your fridge. The kitchen paper will continue to draw moisture from the leaves and keep the leaves fresh for 3–4 days.

WASHING VEGETABLES One method of super-cleaning fruit and veg (other than just giving a quick scrub under a running tap) is soaking it in a solution of 1 tbsp of baking soda plus 1 tbsp of cider vinegar or lemon juice per litre of water, let it sit for 10–20 minutes and then rinse it well.

REVIVING WILTED VEG More robust items such as carrots, radishes, beetroot, celery, asparagus, Swiss chard and flat leaf parsley can be brought back from a softened, wrinkled state to crisp firmness by placing in a bowl of water in the fridge overnight. It re-hydrates them brilliantly. Alternatively, stand things like celery, rhubarb and carrots in a big jar of water.

STOPPING FRUIT AND VEG DISCOLOURING Apples, pears and avocado can sometimes discolour quickly and I've always dipped them in lemon juice to prevent this. However, I now just spray them with a very fine mist of water or briefly dip them into a bowl of water. The water acts as a barrier to prevent air getting to the cut surface to oxidize and discolour it.

SQUEEZING LEMONS If squeezing using a lemon reamer or traditional lemon squeezer, first roll the fruit on a hard surface, pressing gently with the palm of your hand as you do so. This breaks down some of the cell walls and makes it easier to release the juice once the fruit is cut. If you're serving lemons to squeeze over at the table cut each lemon in half diagonally, for ease of handling.

CITRUS ZESTING If you're using a citrus fruit just for its juice, zest it first (particularly if it's an unwaxed, organic fruit) and freeze the zest in a zip-lock bag for future use. Citrus zest has a zingy bitterness and pleasing texture and enhances not only salad dressings but chocolate, tomato sauces, ice creams, custards and pastry. I personally like to run whole lemons (rind, pith, flesh and all) through my juicer as it gives a super-powerful tasting lemon 'juice' to add to green juices, hot toddies and salad dressings, or pour over steamed greens or smoky barbecued meats.

CHOPPING HERBS If you need a larger quantity of a fresh soft-leaf herb one of the easiest ways to do this (rather than painstakingly plucking all the leaves from the stems) is to gather the stems into a bunch, hold the bunch in one hand and with a large sharp knife in the other 'shave' the leaves and tender stems from the bunch.

TRANSPORTING SALADS If you plan on taking your salad any distance it's a good idea to layer it with the heaviest/wettest ingredients on the bottom and the more delicate and drier things on the top. Or, if it's a larger quantity salad, then take all the ingredients separately in zip-lock bags to prevent the different elements getting squashed. Always take the dressing separately too (small jam jars are ideal for this) and dress your salad at the last minute. If you regularly eat salads at work, keep a handy-sized bottle of dressing or balsamic in your desk drawer.

BLANCHING If you're blanching veg to serve in a salad, such as green beans, broad beans or broccoli florets, then resist the temptation to 'refresh' them under cold water as this waterlogs them and prevents them soaking up a dressing. Just cook them for a slightly shorter time, drain them well and place on tea towels topped with kitchen paper and place somewhere cool. Then when they've cooled down either dress them separately or add them to your salad.

SOAKING SEEDS To maximize the health benefits of nuts and seeds soak them first in a bowl of water, ideally overnight. Some require longer soaking than others (there are plenty of guidelines for this on the internet) but by doing so it kicks off the germination process and starts to unlock much of the stored nutrition, along with enzymes that aid their digestion. Rinse and drain nuts and seeds well after soaking and if you want to go a stage further then try sprouting, see opposite. The soaking process makes the nuts and seeds softer and easier to digest and also easier to blend if you're making a nut- or seed-based dressing.

SPROUTING SEEDS There are some nuts, seeds and beans that are better for sprouting than others. You can even sprout seeds in a jam jar in your backpack if you're travelling, so you're never without a boost of nutrition to add to a meal.

MAKING DATE PASTE This makes an excellent raw alternative to sugar or sugar substitutes. Place 8 pitted Medjool dates in a small bowl with just enough water to cover, soak for 2–3 hours (or overnight). Remove the dates from the water and blend in a high-speed blender with a couple of tablespoons of the soaking water to form a thick paste. Thin down with more soaking water if you prefer a runnier 'syrup' consistency. Store in an airtight container in the fridge for up to 2 weeks.

INFUSING VINEGARS These are really simple to make and you can use a wide variety of ingredient combinations for flavouring, such as rosemary, orange, lemon, fennel, star anise, oregano, marjoram, tarragon, shallot, horseradish, garlic, thyme and raspberry. To do this, wash and dry your flavouring ingredients well, chop up smaller if necessary and divide between 2 x 500ml sterilized glass jars. Heat 1 litre of white vinegar in a large saucepan until it's just barely simmering then pour into the two jars leaving a little space at the top. Screw on airtight lids and store in a cool dark place for 2–4 weeks. You can leave the flavouring ingredients in the jar as you use up the vinegar (the flavour will get stronger over time) or discard them. Keep refrigerated once opened.

Alternatively, for a non-heated version, just add your flavourings to a bottle of vinegar and leave to infuse for 10–12 days. The flavour will be much more subtle than the heated vinegar method but still distinctive.

INFUSING OILS For instant flavoured herb oil just place a handful of fresh herbs in the bowl of a food processor fitted with an 'S' blade and pour over enough good-quality oil to cover. Blend until the herbs are finely chopped or blitzed into the oil completely. You can then use straight away or store in an airtight container in the fridge. If you want a clear oil then strain well before using or bottling.

SUPER-CHARGING YOUR SALAD If you want to super-charge your salad try adding in a few super-food ingredients, such as goji berries, chia seeds, nuts and seeds or add a super-food powder (such as spirulina, baobab or cacao) to your dressing.

KITCHEN KIT

To make a salad you need nothing more than a sharp knife and a cutting board.

A simple box grater and a veg peeler are handy to have, and to make dressings a jam jar and a measuring spoon will do the trick... BUT if you fancy getting a little more creative then with a few extra implements you can really have some fun. These are the tools I like to use:

* high-speed blender with different size jars

* super-sharp mandolins

* microplane graters with different blades for zesting and coarse grating

* whisks – a small one for everyday use and a large balloon whisk

* aerolatte (for making foamy dressings)

* melon baller (a standard-sized one, a mini melon baller and an oval-shaped one)

* selection of sharp knives – a large chopping knife and smaller knifes for delicate work

* serrated or zig-zag-bladed wave knife

* cannelling knife

* basic vegetable peeler

* julienne peeler

* vegetable pencil sharpeners (for making shavings and ruffles)

* lemon zester (for zesting lemons and decorative scoring)

* spiralizers – a standard one and one for making angel hair strands

* various cutters (cookie, pastry and veg cutters, and a pasta wheel)

* food processor with grating discs, slicing discs, an 'S' blade and a citrus press

* sprouter for home-sprouted seeds and beans

* lemon juicer and reamer

* various measuring jugs and spoons

CUTTING TECHNIQUES

Most fruit and veg are exceptionally delicious raw, and when very finely sliced (or shaved paper-thin) even the more fibrous ones become easy and palatable to eat. Using different styles of cutting and chopping adds interest and variety from a visual and textural point of view, and you can greatly enhance the appeal of a dish with just a few simple techniques.

The way you cut a fruit or vegetable can also influence its flavour in a dish, for instance some strong-tasting ingredients, such as onion or fennel, if sliced very finely have a much less dominant taste than if they were cut into large chunks. So it's worth bearing this in mind when you prepare a salad.

gaufrette-style
courgettes

mandolin-sliced
sweet potato

ribbon-cut carrot using a
vegetable 'pencil' sharpener

These are the different cutting techniques I like to use, all of which you can find in this book:

❋ **ribbon:** wide, long, fine slices using a vegetable peeler

❋ **spiralize:** thick noodles, fine noodles, angel hair noodles or ruffles using a spiralizer

❋ **mandolin:** various thicknesses using different blades

❋ **julienne:** cut by hand or with a julienne peeler into long, thin slices

❋ **dice:** cut into small squares

❋ **chiffonade:** shredded or finely sliced – perfect for leafy greens and herbs

❋ **allumette:** short and long matchsticks

❋ **baton:** long, thin, rectangular shape

❋ **crinkle-cut:** also zig-zags (thick and thin), wavy-edged dice, or gaufrette-style waffles using a serrated wave knife

❋ **balls:** melon ball size, mini melon balls, oval balls

❋ **cookie-cut shapes:** stars, squares, hearts

❋ **riced:** use a box grater or food processor – perfect for cauliflower or broccoli florets

❋ **shred:** cut by hand, vegetable peeler or grater

❋ **grate:** coarse, medium or fine

zig-zag cut   julienne-cut   mandolin-sliced   cookie cutter
candy beetroot   spring onion   yellow pepper   cut carrot slices

salads
&
slaws

AVOCADO 'TRUFFLE' SALAD

Avocado can be used to make savoury 'truffles', which look interesting in a salad or can be speared on to cocktail sticks to serve as a canapé. Here, I've simply scooped out the avocado flesh with a melon baller and rolled the balls in a mixture of seeds to give an extra super-food boost to the salad.

A light vinaigrette dressing, such as the Herb Vinaigrette (see page 126) or Grilled Citrus Dressing (see page 129), adds a mildly acidic balance to the richness of the avocado and will lightly coat the delicate salad leaves, rather than weigh them down.

2 large handfuls of mixed green salad leaves
3–4 tablespoons mixed seeds, such as sesame, hemp and poppy seeds
2–3 large ripe avocados
1 small handful of sprouted seeds
Herb Vinaigrette (see page 126) or
Grilled Citrus Dressing (see page 129)
1 small handful of edible flowers, to garnish

Avocado provides healthy monounsaturated fat and vitamin E, which protects cells from damage. But take care if you're watching your waistline as they can provide quite a few calories!

Place the salad leaves in a shallow serving bowl. Put the seeds in a separate small bowl.

Cut the avocados in half and remove the stones. Using a melon baller, scoop out balls of avocado or cut the flesh into large cubes. Roll the avocado pieces in the seeds until coated and place on top of the leaves.

Scatter over the sprouted seeds and either serve straightaway or cover and store in the fridge for up to a day or two. As the avocado is coated in seeds the flesh won't oxidize and turn brown.

Pour your dressing of choice over the salad and scatter over the edible flowers just before serving.

Instead of the avocado...
Roll balls of soft or semi-soft cheese in a mixture of seeds and herbs.

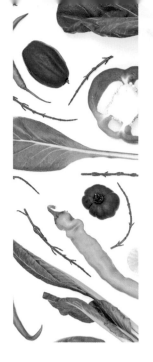

BOK CHOY & SAMPHIRE SALAD

Samphire (sea asparagus) is a wonderfully nutritious vegetable that grows in coastal parts of Britain and is delicious to eat raw. It's tender and succulent yet crunchy, and has a gentle salty taste. It's best to buy it as fresh as you can and if you can't get hold of any, substitute it with other edible fresh sea vegetables such as arame, sea palm or dulse.

I've used it in this crispy mixed salad with bok choy and peppers and dressed it simply with lime juice and a little fresh green chilli. A sweet and spicy vinaigrette would also work well, such as the Sweet & Sour Dressing (see page 84).

Sea vegetables, like samphire, are a very rich source of iodine – a mineral that's vital in the production of thyroid hormones that control metabolic rate.

400g (14oz) samphire or other edible
fresh sea vegetables, trimmed
2 large bok choy or choy sum
4–5 mixed peppers (green, red, orange or yellow)
1 green chilli
finely grated zest and juice of 3 limes

Wash the samphire well and chop the stems and leaves of the bok choy.

Deseed the peppers and chop into small dice or slices (or a combination of the two). Deseed the green chilli and finely chop.

Put the samphire, bok choy and peppers into a bowl or on a platter and squeeze over the lime juice before sprinkling over the lime zest and chopped chilli.

Also try with...
Any fish or seafood would team well with this salad, such as fresh tuna steaks, prawns or salmon.

As an alternative to the samphire, try lightly steamed or roasted asparagus.

FIG & POMEGRANATE SALAD

Figs are great in a salad – they look pretty and have a gentle sweetness and soft texture. They are also one of the truly seasonal fruits that don't seem to be available all year round, so are a treat to look forward to come late summer.

This salad is based on rich, deep colours with the glistening flesh of the figs and sparkling pomegranate seeds giving it a jewel-like quality.

2 red leaf lettuces
1 Little Gem or 4 Romaine lettuce leaves
6–8 large figs
$\frac{1}{4}$–$\frac{1}{2}$ red onion, peeled
2–3 pomegranates

Figs are a very good non-dairy source of bone-friendly calcium, plus gram for gram they have more iron than steak!

Tear both types of lettuce into bite-sized pieces. Cut the figs into quarters or thick slices and very finely slice the red onion.

To remove the seeds from the pomegranates, cut them in half then, placing your hand over a large bowl, hold one half of a pomegranate with the cut-side facing downwards and bash the outside with a rolling pin. The seeds should easily dislodge and be captured in the palm of your hand with the juices falling into the bowl. (Wear an apron to do this as the juices can splatter!) Repeat with the remaining pomegranate halves.

Put all the salad ingredients in a bowl, gently toss together then arrange on a serving platter, pouring over any pomegranate juice in the bowl.

Try this...

The figs and onions can be roasted to give this salad a new twist. It's also great with fresh creamy cheeses, or as a side dish to game or smoked fish.

A handful of honey-roasted or spiced nuts would be a nice addition, too.

BROCCOLI & SPROUT SALAD WITH CAPERBERRIES & OLIVES

Broccoli and Brussels sprouts are great in raw salads as their robust structure means you can shave or slice them really thinly and they still keep their texture and bite. They're also fairly bland in flavour so pair well with strong-tasting ingredients such as the spring onions, capers, caperberries and olives in this dish.

If Brussels sprouts are out of season, white or green cabbage work just as well; after all, sprouts are just like mini cabbages.

300g (10½oz) Brussels sprouts
2–3 spring onions, trimmed
1 head of broccoli
100g (3½oz) preserved pitted green or black olives
70g (2½oz) preserved capers and/or caperberries
2 tablespoons pickling liquid from the jar of olives or capers
1 tablespoon cold-pressed extra virgin olive oil
3 tablespoons hemp seeds, or any other seeds
salt and pepper

By combining a powerful duo of cruciferous veg – broccoli and Brussels sprouts – this salad will bump up your intake of folate and vitamin C.

Finely slice or shave the Brussels sprouts into wafer-thin slices and chop the spring onions (both the white and green parts).

Break the broccoli into florets then finely chop them in a food processor, or you could cut the florets into small pieces with a knife.

Mix the broccoli, Brussels sprouts and spring onions together in a bowl and add the olives, capers and caperberries, chopping some before adding, if desired.

Make a quick dressing using the pickling liquid from the olives or capers and whisking it together with the olive oil and some seasoning. Pour the dressing over the salad, mix well and sprinkle over the hemp seeds before serving.

Give it some crisp...
- A scattering of crumbled crispy, smoky bacon or pancetta gives this salad an extra savoury depth of flavour.
- The outside leaves of the Brussels sprouts are great roasted until crisp and then sprinkled over the top to add contrast to the finely shaved raw ones.

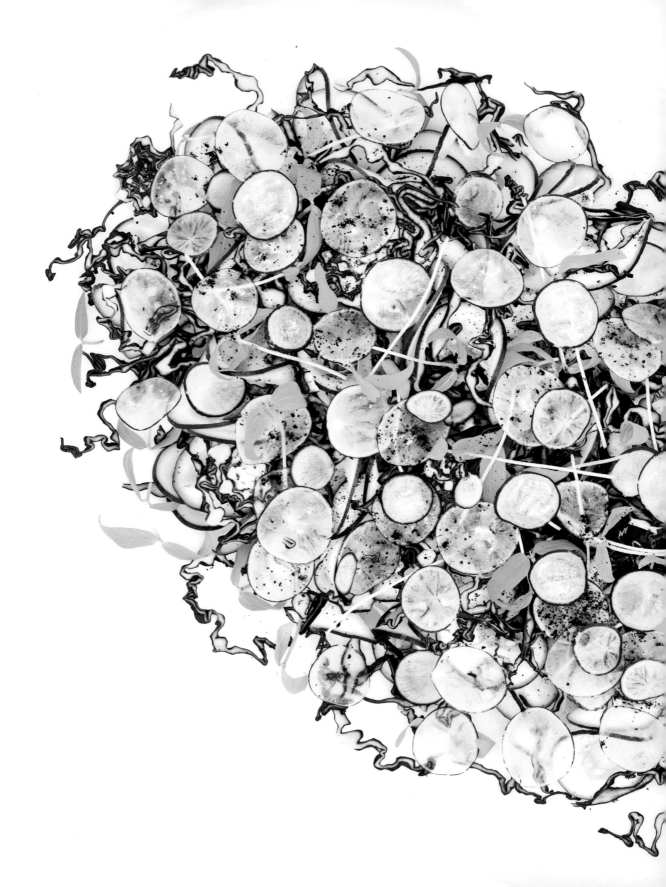

RED CABBAGE & COURGETTE RUFFLE SALAD

Deep purple in colour, the acai berry (normally sold in powdered form) is classed as a super-food. The powder makes a dramatic coloured Acai Berry Dressing (see page 135) for this salad, or you can just sprinkle some of the powder over the top, as I have done here.

I cut the courgette into large ruffle shapes using one of the discs on my spiralizer and, if you want to keep the salad 100 per cent raw, you could substitute the pomegranate molasses for date paste or a sweetener of your choice.

Acai is famed for its anthocyanin antioxidant content and is a source of vitamin E, which scavenges the free radicals that damage cells.

3 courgettes, trimmed
$\frac{1}{2}$ red cabbage
3–4 radishes, trimmed
Acai Berry Dressing (see page 135)
1 handful of mixed sprouted seeds

Using a spiralizer, cut the courgettes into ruffles or 'noodles', or simply grate them using a box grater instead.

Finely slice the cabbage and the radishes and arrange all the salad ingredients on a serving platter or in a bowl.

Pour the acai berry dressing over the salad. It is quite dark and sinister in colour, so if you mix it into the salad you'll have a spooky-looking dish! Sprinkle over the sprouted seeds before serving.

For a cooked alternative...
Braise the cabbage first and add to the salad with a handful of chopped sultanas and maybe a little chopped crispy smoked bacon.

RADISH, BEETROOT & ORANGE SALAD

This is a lovely fresh-tasting salad to make in the winter months when blood oranges are in season. And if you can get hold of yellow beetroot as well as red, this salad is even more aesthetically pleasing.

Cutting the beetroot, red onion and fennel into wafer-thin slices makes them more digestible when eaten raw. If you don't like the pungency of raw onion, leave it to marinate in the lemony dressing for 30 minutes and its flavour will soften significantly.

3 blood oranges
2 raw red beetroots, scrubbed or peeled
2 raw yellow or golden beetroots, scrubbed or peeled
5–6 radishes, trimmed
$\frac{1}{4}$–$\frac{1}{2}$ red onion, peeled
1 fennel bulb
1 handful of edible flowers or herbs, to garnish

> Fennel is a traditional stomach soother, and beetroot – a good source of iron, folate and nitrates – has been shown to help lower blood pressure.

LEMON DRESSING
finely grated zest and juice of 1 lemon
2 tablespoons extra virgin olive oil
salt and pepper

Remove the pith and skin from the oranges and slice the flesh into segments. It's a good idea to do this over a bowl to collect any juices.

Very finely slice both types of beetroots, the radishes, red onion and fennel (it's great if you have a mandolin to do this, or use the slicing disk on a food processor, or cut by hand with a sharp knife). Place the vegetable slices in a large bowl with the orange segments.

To make the dressing, whisk together the lemon zest and juice with the olive oil and seasoning in a bowl. Mix in some of the orange juice, if you like.

Pour the dressing over the salad and mix gently with your hands. Transfer the salad to a serving platter and scatter over a few edible flowers or herbs.

For a cooked alternative...

Roast the beetroot in a hot oven (wrapped in foil for about 1 hour or until tender) and then peel and slice when cooled. The fennel and radishes can be roasted, too. Cut the fennel into 1cm ($\frac{1}{2}$in) thick slices and keep the radishes whole. Lightly coat the veg in cold-pressed extra virgin olive oil, season, and roast for 25–30 minutes until tender. Add to the salad when cooled to room temperature.

SUMMER SQUASH SALAD

This pretty salad, made with paper-thin shavings of raw courgette and summer squash combined with pea shoots and edible flowers, is pepped up with a herby Gremolata-style Dressing (see page 133).

I've used yellow and green courgettes and patty pan squash but any varieties will do, just as long as they're reasonably young, small and tender and not too watery.

2–3 courgettes, a mixture of green and yellow, trimmed
2–3 summer squash, such as patty pan
1 handful of pea shoots
Gremolata-style Dressing (see page 133)
1 handful of edible flowers, to garnish

Courgettes are a good source of potassium and folate, while pea shoots provide high levels of vitamin C and vitamin A.

Very thinly slice the courgettes using a mandolin or speed peeler. Repeat with the summer squash then tip everything into a serving bowl or on to a serving platter. Scatter over the pea shoots.

Serve the salad with the dressing poured over the top, or separately on the side. Scatter over the edible flowers just before serving.

For a light meal...

Serve this summery salad with low-fat protein foods, such as cottage cheese, poached salmon, skinless chicken or turkey breast, or edamame beans – it's perfect for those following a clean, paleo diet.

Cooling and refreshing, the salad would also make a good side dish to barbecued food or smoked fish.

AVOCADO, TOMATO & LETTUCE SALAD

Avocado, tomato and lettuce work really well together in a salad, and if your avocado is really ripe you can mush it up into a guacamole-type dressing.

It's best to make this when tomatoes are at the peak of their season so they're really flavoursome and need little extra help in that department other than a sprinkle of sea salt and maybe a swig of good quality cold-pressed extra virgin olive oil.

I love using different varieties of tomatoes and here I've suggested the large Coeur de Boeuf and the tiny Tomberry.

Tomatoes are packed with lycopene, and avocados with vitamin E. Studies suggest these two nutrients work together in reducing the cell damage that's linked with diseases such as heart disease and cancer.

2–3 avocados
1 large butterhead lettuce
300–400g (10½oz–14oz) mixed tomatoes, such as Coeur de Boeuf and Tomberry
cold-pressed extra virgin olive oil, for drizzling
salt and pepper

Halve, peel, remove the stones and dice the avocados then tear the lettuce into bite-sized pieces.

Chop the tomatoes into chunks or cut into slices, reserving any juices that remain on the chopping board to use to dress the salad.

Combine all the ingredients in a bowl, adding the juices from the tomatoes. Season to taste and add a drizzle of olive oil.

Other meal ideas...

Goats' cheese or any soft, creamy, salty cheese pairs well with the flavours of this salad. It also makes a great sandwich filling.

Sprinkle over some hemp seeds for extra vegan protein, or serve as a side dish to a vegetarian omelette.

WALDORF SALAD

This is a version of the summertime classic, with the traditional mayonnaise replaced with a creamy Raw Cashew Mayo (see page 131).

I've used red-skinned apples, here, and sliced them with a serrated wave knife to give a pretty crinkle-cut edge.

1 large handful of seedless red grapes
1 large handful of seedless green grapes
3–4 celery sticks, trimmed
2 red-skinned apples
1 large handful of walnut halves
Raw Cashew Mayo (see page 131)
celery leaves, fennel fronds or dill, to garnish

Iron and omega-3 are two nutrients that can be difficult to get from a vegan diet, but this salad provides good amounts of both thanks to the cashews and walnuts.

De-stem and halve both types of grapes and finely slice the celery sticks.

Core the apples and cut them into julienne strips or thin slices.

Place the grapes, celery and apple into a large serving bowl with the walnut halves. Pour over half of the raw cashew mayo and mix the salad gently to combine all the ingredients.

Scatter a few celery leaves or fronds of fennel or dill over the top. Serve the remainder of the vegan mayonnaise by the side, or keep for another day.

For a meaty twist...
Anchovies, crispy bacon or poached or roasted chicken all team well with this salad.

PINK RADISH, BEET & YELLOW PEPPER SALAD

This vibrant pink and yellow salad is crisp, sweet and crunchy. The watermelon radishes can be substituted with regular or English Breakfast radishes, and you could use yellow or red beetroot instead of the candy beetroot, if you prefer.

The pale green flecks of the Herby Ranch Dressing (see page 131) look pretty with the colours of this salad, but you could also try the Moroccan Dressing (see page 134), which is flavoured with ras-el-hanout.

2 large raw candy beetroots, scrubbed or peeled
1 large watermelon radish, trimmed
1 small yellow courgette, trimmed
1 small green courgette, trimmed
2 yellow or orange bell peppers
Herby Ranch Dressing (see page 131) or
Moroccan Dressing (see page 134)
1 small handful of mixed herbs, such as oregano,
dill and bronze fennel fronds
1 small handful of edible flowers, such as violets,
borage and sage flowers
salt and pepper

The beetroot and potassium-packed veg in this salad can help keep your blood pressure healthy. And yellow peppers have over twice the vitamin C content of oranges, helping to keep your immune system healthy, too.

Very thinly slice the candy beetroots, watermelon radish and courgettes using a sharp knife or mandolin.

Deseed the peppers and thinly slice into rings.

Arrange the salad ingredients on a serving platter or in a bowl and pour over your dressing of choice. Season and scatter over the fresh herbs and edible flowers just before serving.

Protein boost...
Serve this salad with barbecued meats, or pan-fried or smoked fish.

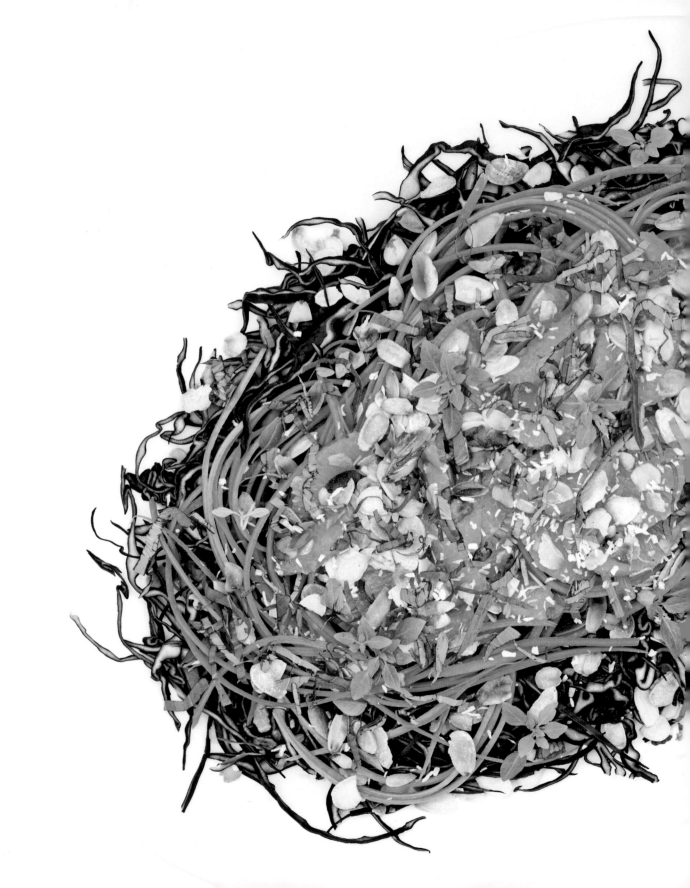

CARROT, ORANGE & RED CABBAGE

Carrot and orange have a natural flavour affinity and when combined with red cabbage they make for an eye-catching colour combination.

I lightly toasted the flaked almonds for the photograph so they'd stand out in the picture, but you can keep them untoasted. If you're making this dish ahead of time, leave adding the almonds to the last minute.

If you're using organic carrots and they come with their green tops, wash a few fronds then finely chop and scatter them over the finished dish.

½ large red cabbage
3–4 large carrots (I often use a mix of orange and purple ones), scrubbed or peeled
3 oranges
100g (3½oz) flaked almonds
1 small handful of roughly chopped parsley or torn basil leaves

This salad supplies all of your daily vitamin A needs! Almonds add some healthy fat, plus calcium, magnesium and iron, too.

Finely slice the red cabbage and slice, grate or cut the carrots into ribbons using a vegetable peeler. Put the vegetables in a serving bowl or on a serving platter.

Finely grate the zest of the oranges, then cut away the peel and pith and segment the flesh, discarding the white membrane. If you do this over the bowl of vegetables, the juice will be amalgamated into the salad and act as a light dressing.

Place the orange segments in the bowl or serving platter and scatter over the flaked almonds and herbs.

Protein boost...

Barbecued fish, diced marinated tempeh or a handful of cooked black beans would all add valuable protein to this salad, and taste good too.

CAULI-FLOWER SALAD

There's been something of a cauliflower revolution in recent years and the once quietly humble vegetable has been thrust into the culinary spotlight, becoming a new darling of the kitchen and many a restaurant menu. The cauliflower's low-carb properties and mild taste make it a brilliant and plausible replacement for rice, potatoes and starchy grains, and there seems to be boundless love for its magical role as a pizza crust.

Thickly cut slices of cauliflower can be pan-cooked or roasted in the oven to make great 'steaks' and oven-roasted, spice-dusted florets make a transformative side dish or snack. However, raw is when it really shines. Grated by hand or in a food processor, it looks like grains of 'rice' and makes a great base for salads. As it is quite bland in flavour a really punchy dressing such as the Moroccan Dressing (see page 134) or Rose Harissa Dressing (see page 129) make good pairings.

Here, I've used purple cauliflower and green romanesco (a cauliflower/broccoli hybrid) as I love the combination of colours. I've also added some raw okra for added crunch and a few edible flowers for prettiness.

Cauliflower is a good source of vitamin C and folate, plus it's part of the cruciferous group of veg thought to have cancer-protective properties.

1 small cauliflower
1 small romanesco
4–5 okra
Moroccan Dressing (see page 134) or
Rose Harissa Dressing (see page 129)
1 handful of edible flowers, to garnish

Cut away the outside leaves from the cauliflower and romanesco, but keep any small tender leaves as these can be 'riced' with the florets. Break into large florets and either coarsely grate or finely chop in a food processor. If using a food processor, be careful not to over-process as the vegetables can soon become mushy. Tip the 'riced' cauliflower and romanesco into a bowl or on a platter.

Thinly slice the okra and scatter it over the 'rice'. Pour your dressing of choice over the salad and top with the edible flowers just before serving.

Low-carb alternative...
This makes a healthy substitute to regular white or brown rice.

BEETROOT CARPACCIO

I have made this salad before with dark, reddy-brown beetroot, which when thinly sliced looks remarkably similar to carpaccio made with beef or salami, but I couldn't resist using candy beetroot, here.

For the matchstick veg, I used sweet potatoes, pink Chinese radish and yellow squash, but any colourful vegetables that slice easily, hold their shape, and you can eat raw will do.

A great dressing to serve with this would be the Sun-dried Tomato Dressing (see page 129) and, for any omnivores, the Crispy Smoky Bacon Dressing (see page 127)

A source of iron and folate, this beetroot salad is also a good choice if you're trying to keep your blood pressure in check.

1 large raw candy beetroot, scrubbed or peeled
2 large pink Chinese radishes or 3–4 regular radishes, trimmed
1–2 apple-sized yellow squash or yellow courgettes, trimmed
2 large sweet potatoes, peeled
cold-pressed extra virgin olive oil or Sun-dried Tomato
Dressing (see page 129), or Crispy Smoky Bacon Dressing
(see page 127)

Thinly slice the candy beetroot and chop the other vegetables into long, thin matchsticks.

Drizzle a little olive oil over the candy beetroot for a glistening effect or mix all together with the dressing of your choice.

Try this...
Parmesan shavings are lovely sprinkled over this salad.
You could also roast the vegetable matchsticks to make a bed of crispy vegetable chips.

LITTLE GEM 'TACOS'

Little Gem (or small Romaine) leaves are ideal for making 'tacos'. This salad has an interesting combination of flavours and textures with mild-tasting crisp lettuce, a creamy avocado and sweet red pepper salsa, a tang from the lime, plus a crispy topping of sprouted seeds.

If you want to take this dish to work for lunch or a picnic, the salsa can be easily transported in a screw-top jar. It can also be made in advance and stored in an airtight container in the fridge.

If your avocado is really ripe then you could mush it with the other ingredients to make a kind of guacamole, it will still taste delicious.

2 Little Gem lettuces
1 large handful of sprouted seeds (I used mooli/radish sprouts)
edible rose petals, to garnish
lime wedges, to serve

AVOCADO & RED PEPPER SALSA
finely grated zest and juice of 2 limes
2 ripe avocados
1 red pepper
1 small handful of mild red chillies, or to taste depending on how hot they are and your taste preference
2 spring onions, trimmed
1 small handful of chopped mixed herbs, such as parsley, mint, chives and dill
salt and pepper

Avocado is a great source of heart-healthy monounsaturated fat, while sprouted seeds supply antioxidants, B vitamins and protein.

To make the salsa, pour the lime juice into a bowl. Peel and remove the stones from the avocados and cut into small dice. Add them to the bowl and toss in the lime juice to prevent them discolouring. Deseed the red pepper and chillies and cut them both into small dice, cutting the chillies finer if you prefer. Finely slice the spring onions. Mix all the ingredients together, including the lime zest and herbs, and season with a little salt and pepper.

Gently separate the Little Gem leaves then wash and dry them.

When you are ready to serve, fill each lettuce leaf with a spoonful of the avocado and red pepper salsa and sprinkle over a few sprouted seeds.

Arrange the filled leaves on a platter, scatter over a few fragrant rose petals for a summery look and serve with some extra wedges of lime for squeezing over.

For a protein boost...
Try adding small cubes of marinated tofu or tempeh, or flaked tuna or grilled mackerel.

MIDDLE EASTERN-INSPIRED SUMMER SALAD

Candy beetroots are one of my favourite summer veg and I love their crazily pretty pink and white candy stripes and sweet, mild taste. They're not as juicy as red beetroot (so much easier to prepare raw) and their taste reminds me of a cross between a beetroot and a radish. If you can't get hold of them, substitute with radishes or red or golden beetroot (raw, not cooked).

I like to serve this with the fragrant Moroccan Dressing (see page 134) and a sprinkling of pretty rose petals.

2 crisp lettuces, such as Romaine
2–3 raw candy beetroots and/or raw red or golden beetroot, scrubbed or peeled
1 handful of shelled pistachio nuts
1 handful of pomegranate seeds
Moroccan Dressing (see page 134)
ras-el-hanout and fresh edible rose petals, to garnish

The pistachio nuts and pomegranate seeds give this salad a nutrition kick as together they're a good source of antioxidants, vitamins C and E, fibre and potassium.

Simply tear the lettuce leaves into bite-size pieces.

Slice the beetroots very thinly using a mandolin or vegetable peeler, or carefully cut into wafer-thin slices with a small, sharp knife.

Roughly chop the pistachios and then gently combine all the salad ingredients together in a large bowl.

Pour the Moroccan dressing over the salad and sprinkle a little ras-el-hanout and fresh rose petals over the top to garnish.

Why not try...
Serve with feta or a creamy goats' cheese crumbled over the top.
This would also make a great side dish to chargrilled or barbecued meat.
Try the dressing poured over a couscous salad or a platter of roasted veg.

CRUNCHY CARROT & BEETROOT SALAD

The Raw Cashew Mayo (see page 131) lends a rich creaminess to this salad, while the hazelnuts give it a pleasant savoury crunch. I've toasted the nuts (before crushing them) so they visually stand out, but if you're keeping this salad completely raw then leave them untoasted.

Packed with all the main cell-protective antioxidant vitamins (A, C and E), this salad also provides anaemia-protective iron from the cashews.

3–4 Little Gem lettuces or 1 large Romaine lettuce
2–3 large carrots, scrubbed or peeled
1 large raw red or yellow beetroot, scrubbed or peeled
150g (5½oz) hazelnuts
½ quantity Raw Cashew Mayo (see page 131)
1 small handful of chopped mixed herbs, such as mint, basil and parsley

Tear the lettuce leaves into bite-sized pieces and scatter on a large platter or place in a serving bowl.

Very thinly slice the carrots and beetroot (a mandolin is ideal for this) and crush or chop the hazelnuts.

Add the carrots and beetroot to the lettuce and pour over the raw mayo. Mix the salad together gently with your hands, then scatter over the hazelnuts and herbs before serving.

Top it off with…
a few shavings of Parmesan or dollops of creamy ricotta.

DANDELION, PARSLEY & BERGAMOT

Dandelion or other wild greens are packed with nutritional goodness – just be careful when you pick them that they're not polluted by car fumes or pesticides from nearby fields. Also, wash them very well before use.

If you have room in your garden it's worth cultivating a few dandelions to add variety to salads, and they're really delicious if you grow them in the dark under a plant pot so the leaves are paler and a little less bitter.

Citrus fruit is great to pair with dark leafy greens as its vitamin C content increases the absorption of iron found in the greens. I've used bergamot oranges, which are typically used for their amazing aroma (particularly in the perfume industry). If you can find them they're well worth buying, if only to experience the incredible fragrance when you cut them.

Parsley contains more than double the iron level of red meat and over three times the vitamin C content of oranges.

2–3 large handfuls of dandelion leaves
or other green salad leaves
3–4 large bunches of flat leaf parsley
juice from 2 bergamot oranges or regular oranges

Chop or tear the dandelion leaves into small pieces and cut the parsley leaves away from the stems.

Place the dandelion and parsley in a large bowl and squeeze over the juice from the bergamot oranges.

Bulk it up...
If you want to make this more substantial, add Romaine lettuce and maybe some mango or avocado.

KALE & RADISH SALAD WITH BLUEBERRY DRESSING

I've used white kale in this salad as it's so decorative but the normal green variety is just as good, if a little more strongly flavoured. The watermelon radishes provide a decorative contrast and the vibrant purple colour of the blueberry and cashew dressing adds a dramatic touch as well as a super-food boost. The sweet and creamy dressing also counteracts the slight bitterness of the kale.

300g (10½oz) blueberries
100g (3½oz) cashew nuts
2 large bunches of kale
3–4 watermelon radishes or regular radishes, trimmed
salt and pepper

It's been shown that blueberries can help to relax the walls of blood vessels, potentially reducing the risk of hardened arteries. Cashews are a fab source of iron – especially useful for vegans and vegetarians.

Using a high-speed blender, blend half of the blueberries with the cashew nuts, seasoning, and 100ml (3½fl oz) water until smooth and creamy. You may need to add a little extra water to the dressing to loosen it to a pouring consistency. Set aside until needed.

Tear the leafy parts of the kale away from the stems and chop the leaves very finely.

Thinly slice or shave the radishes and add the kale and the radishes to a serving bowl.

Pour the blueberry and cashew dressing over the salad and scatter the remaining blueberries on top.

Roast, top, juice...
Roast the radishes whole until tender for a nice contrast to the kale sprightliness.
Crumble crispy, smoky bacon or blue cheese on top in place of the dressing.
Juice and drink the kale stems, rather than throwing them away.

EDAMAME BEAN SALAD

Edamame beans are young soya beans that are picked before they start to harden so they're tender and fresh – a bit like young broad beans. They're a great source of protein and are a general all-round nutritional super-food, and are particularly beneficial in a vegan diet.

They're combined here with poppy seed-specked avocado and served on a bed of matchstick carrots (I've used purple, orange and yellow carrots).

Any citrus or creamy dressing, or the spicy Rose Harissa Dressing (see page 129) would work well with this salad.

3–4 large carrots, scrubbed or peeled
1–2 ripe avocados
2 tablespoons poppy seeds
300g (10½oz) shelled edamame beans
dressing of choice

You've got to love edamame – these beans provide a complete source of protein, along with healthy, slow-release carbohydrate and fibre. Teamed with the vitamin-rich veg they make a salad that's a balanced meal in its own right.

Cut the carrots into fine matchsticks (there's no need to peel them if they are organic) using a mandolin or julienne peeler, or coarsely grate them – they'll taste just as good. Place them in a serving bowl.

Halve, peel and remove the stones of the avocados, then cut the flesh into large chunks. Put the avocado chunks in a bowl and lightly coat in the poppy seeds.

Place the edamame and avocado on top of the carrots, pour over the dressing of your choice and mix well to combine.

Protein boost…
Seared, poached or barbecued salmon goes well with this salad.
For a vegetarian addition, try a poached or runny fried egg on top.

MIXED TOMATO & HERB SALAD

This salad is lovely to make in the summer when there's an abundance of ripe tomatoes and garden herbs. I like to dress it simply with a little olive oil and a squeeze of lemon juice and seasoning.

As the ingredients are all quite delicate you can drizzle over the simple dressing as you assemble the salad: first add a layer of chopped tomatoes to your bowl with a few green leaves, then add a drizzle of olive oil, a little squeeze of lemon or lime juice and some seasoning, then repeat with some more tomatoes, leaves, dressing...

To make the salad more substantial and boost its nutritional content, you could add a few handfuls of chopped young kale leaves and slices of cucumber. I like to cut grooves into the skin of the cucumber to give it a pretty frilly edge when sliced.

If you prefer a more substantial dressing, then the Pistachio Pesto (see page 132) would work really well.

400–500g (14oz–1lb 2oz) ripe tomatoes
200g (7oz) baby green leaf salad
1 large handful of chopped mixed herbs, such parsley, dill and chives
1 tablespoon cold-pressed extra virgin olive oil
1 lemon or lime
salt and pepper

This salad provides lots of healthy lycopene (from the tomatoes) and the olive oil will help this fat-soluble antioxidant to be better absorbed.

Roughly chop the tomatoes and tear any larger salad leaves into bite-sized pieces.

Layer the tomatoes, salad leaves and herbs in a serving bowl, drizzling a little olive oil and adding a squeeze of lemon or lime juice between each layer as you go. Season to taste.

Protein boost...
Serve this salad with poached white fish or seared tuna. Sun-dried tomatoes, roasted peppers, ricotta cheese, mozzarella or burrata also make lovely additions.

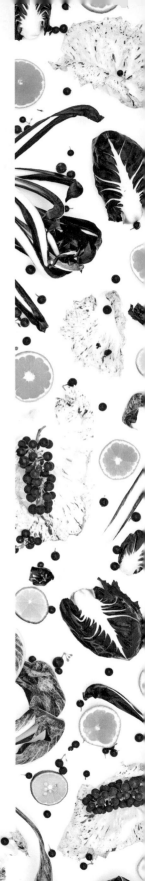

RADICCHIO & PICKLED GRAPE SALAD

I've used three different types of radicchio in this salad. The pretty, deep red colours of the rossa di Verona and spear-like leaves of the treviso contrast visually with the cream and pale pink specked castelfranco. The crisp, bitter leaves are tempered with a zesty orange vinaigrette and little bursts of spicy sweetness from the pickled grapes.

This salad supplies plenty of immune-enhancing vitamin C and some fibre. Bitter radicchio leaves are a good source of folate and antioxidants.

2 handfuls of small seedless black grapes
3 different radicchio, including treviso, castelfranco and rossa di Verona
2 tablespoons cold-pressed extra virgin olive oil
salt and pepper

PICKLING LIQUID
finely grated zest and juice of 1 orange
2 tablespoons raw apple cider vinegar
1 tablespoon date paste or sweetener of your choice
2 star anise
a pinch of fennel seeds
a pinch of red chilli flakes
1 teaspoon salt

Place the pickling liquid ingredients (except the orange zest) in a bowl with 3 tablespoons water and stir until combined.

Stir the grapes into the pickling liquid and leave at room temperature for 30 minutes or in the fridge overnight.

Tear the radicchio into bite-sized pieces and place in a serving bowl. Remove the grapes from the pickling liquid (reserving the liquid) and scatter them over the leaves.

Put 2–3 tablespoons of the pickling liquid, the reserved orange zest and olive oil in a bowl and whisk to combine. Season to taste, and pour the dressing over the salad.

· · · ·

Perfect pairings...
Pair with roast duck. The slightly bitter radicchio plus the sweetness of the orange dressing and the piquant pickled grapes cut through the fattiness of the meat. Top with spiced caramelized nuts, crumbled blue cheese or a poached egg.

RAINBOW CHARD & BLACK RADISH SALAD

This is quite a masculine-looking salad – if there is such a thing! The strong, dark colours of the Swiss chard contrast with the bright white flesh of the black-skinned radishes (or black mooli), while the fiery kick from the Ginger & Wasabi Dressing (see page 134) make it a very 'purposeful' dish.

Swiss chard supplies vitamin A and magnesium, a mineral that can help contribute to a reduction in tiredness and fatigue.

2 bunches of Swiss chard
1 large black radish, trimmed
Ginger & Wasabi Dressing (see page 134)

Tear the chard leaves away from the stems. Place the leaves on top of each other, then roll them up lengthways into a cigar shape and cut into thin slices, chiffonade-style. Place the leaves in a bowl, separating the strands as you go.

Cut the black radish into matchsticks by first cutting it into thin discs, then stacking them on top of each other before slicing into thin sticks. Scatter these over the sliced chard leaves.

Pour the ginger and wasabi dressing over the salad just before serving.

For meat-eaters and veggies...
Barbecued meat or roast beef would go well with this salad, while a veggie burger would make a tasty addition for vegetarians.

MASSAGED KALE SALAD WITH ORANGES & CRANBERRIES

By massaging a dressing into the kale leaves you help to break down the tough fibres until they become soft and silky. The sweet orange dressing works well with the slightly bitter kale.

I've combined the kale with some finely chopped white cabbage for extra crunch and oranges and dried cranberries for sweetness. A few finely sliced fresh cranberries also add texture and a gentle tartness.

Nutrient-packed kale (rich in lutein, folate, iron and vitamin A) teams here with proanthocyanidin-rich cranberries, which are a traditional remedy for urinary tract infections.

3 large oranges
2–3 tablespoons cold-pressed extra virgin olive oil
1 large bunch of kale, such as cavolo nero (dino kale)
100g (3½oz) fresh cranberries
50g (1¾oz) dried cranberries
salt and pepper

Finely grate the zest of the oranges, then cut away the peel and pith and segment the flesh, discarding the white membrane. It's best to do this over a bowl to catch any juices. Whisk together 1–2 tablespoons of the orange juice in the bowl with the zest, olive oil and some seasoning to make a dressing.

Tear the leafy parts of the kale away from the stems and remove any tough veins in the leaves. Tear the leaves into 2.5–5cm (1–2in) pieces and place them in a large bowl.

Pour the orange dressing over the kale and start to massage and scrunch the leaves with your fingers – it will take a while for the leaves to yield but they will gradually start to soften and become more pliable and tender. They are done when they're feeling silky soft.

Thinly slice the fresh cranberries and roughly chop the dried cranberries and add them to the kale with the orange segments.

Leave for 30 minutes or overnight in the fridge for the flavours to mingle and develop. Mix again before serving to distribute any juices in the bottom of the dish.

● Protein boost...
● Rich-tasting protein foods, such as roast salmon or poached eggs,
● work well with the bitterness of the kale and the sweet and sour
● acidity of the oranges and cranberries.

COURGETTE 'NOODLE' & OLIVE SALAD

I love all the different green-on-green colours of this salad and if you're a fan of capers and olives the incorporated dressing is a real treat.

The strong flavours of the dressing work well with the neutral-tasting courgettes and the shower of grated cauliflower gives the visual impression of grated Parmesan cheese as well as a pleasant texture.

3–4 courgettes, trimmed
100–150g (3½–5½oz) preserved green olives
50g (1¾oz) preserved capers
finely grated zest and juice of 1 lemon
1 handful of mixed soft-leaf herbs, such as basil, dill, mint and parsley
1 garlic clove, peeled
2 tablespoons cold-pressed extra virgin olive oil
1 large cauliflower floret

This salad provides plenty of potassium, folate and some healthy fats, too.

Cut the courgettes into long strands using a julienne peeler or spiralizer and set aside.

Roughly chop half the olives and half the capers by hand (remove the stones first if the olives need pitting) and set aside.

To make the dressing, add the remaining olives and capers to the bowl of a food processor along with the lemon juice, zest, herbs and garlic. Process briefly whilst trickling in the olive oil to make a chunky, salsa verde-type sauce.

Place the courgette 'noodles' in a bowl and pour over the dressing, mixing gently with your hands. Scatter over the chopped olives and capers and grate over a snowy dredge of cauliflower.

Try this...
Anchovies and Parmesan go beautifully with this salad or, for a vegan option, try a sprinkling of nutritional yeast flakes.
The dressing makes a great pasta sauce, while the salad is good with grilled meats.

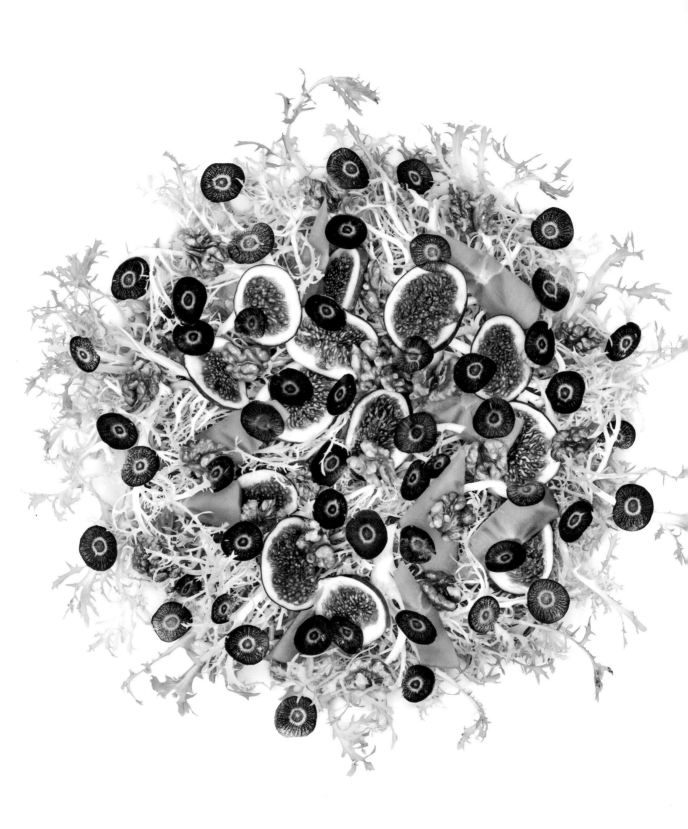

FRISÉE & FIG SALAD

The sweetness of the figs and the Sharon fruit balance out the bitterness of the frisée lettuce in this salad.

If you can, wait until your Sharon fruit ripen fully as they almost turn into a different fruit. It takes a bit of trial and error as you have to leave them until the skins turn brown and they look as though they're about to go bad, but they transform from being soft-textured and mildly sweet to the flesh inside becoming almost jellified with a deep caramelly taste and an incredible depth of perfumed sweetness.

If they aren't fully ripe, use them as they are and moisten the salad with a dressing. A Citrus & Beetroot Dressing (see page 128) or Sweet Smoky Paprika Vinaigrette (see page 127) would both work well.

1 large frisée lettuce
2 large carrots (I used purple ones), scrubbed or peeled
4 ripe figs
3 Sharon fruits (persimmon)
Citrus & Beetroot Dressing (see page 128) or
Sweet Smoky Paprika Vinaigrette (see page 127) (optional)
75g (2¾oz) walnuts

Boost your intake of iron, calcium and vitamin A from the figs and carrots in this delicious salad. Plus, you'll get a source of heart-healthy omega 3 fat from the walnuts.

Tear the frisée leaves into bite-sized pieces and slice or grate the carrots (there's no need to peel them if they're organic).

Slice the figs and chop the Sharon fruit into chunks, unless you're using particularly ripe ones then cut in half and spoon out the flesh.

Combine the ingredients with your dressing of choice, if using, and scatter over the walnuts.

Try this...
The sweetness of the figs and Sharon fruit combined with the slight bitterness of the walnuts and frisée make a great base for the addition of crumbly blue or goats' cheese, seared tuna, Parma ham or crispy pancetta.

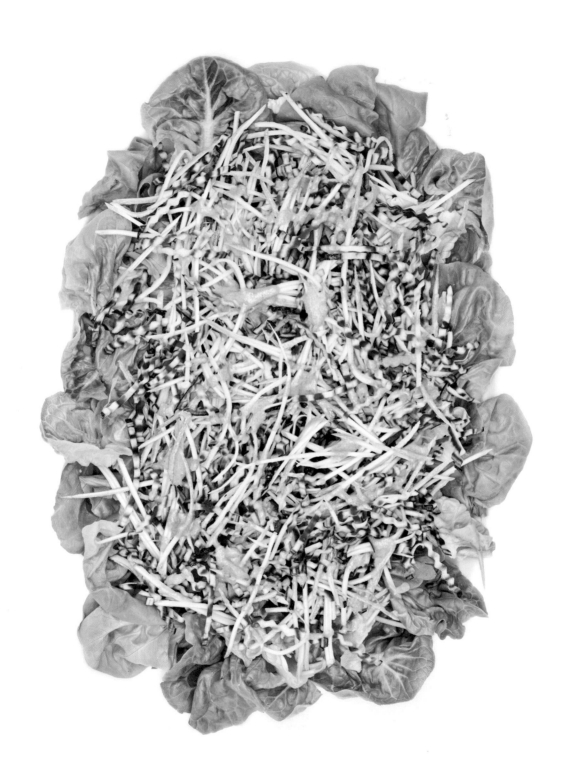

COURGETTE & CANDY BEETROOT SALAD

I confess I have something of an obsession with candy beetroot, as you may have noticed from their prevalence in this book! They're an old heirloom variety, botanically called Chioggia and are much drier in texture than red beetroot, more like a cross between a beetroot and a radish. I love their crazy psychedelic pink and white stripes and they are fun to play around with in a salad as they look so pretty, either thinly sliced across the equator (downwards gives a different effect) or sliced into matchsticks, or zig-zags as I've cut them here.

This salad goes well with the Creamy Turmeric Dressing (see page 135), but you could also try the Peanut Satay Dressing (see page 134) or the Citrus Ginger Dressing (see page 128).

3 Little Gem lettuces or 1 large Romaine lettuce
3–4 courgettes, trimmed
2 large raw candy beetroot, scrubbed or peeled
Creamy Turmeric Dressing (see page 135)

Courgettes are a good provider of potassium – important for maintaining healthy blood pressure.

Tear up the Little Gem or Romaine lettuce leaves and place in a bowl.

Cut the courgettes into fine strands using a julienne peeler, or grate them using the coarse side of a box grater, or you could spiralize them.

Cut the candy beetroot into matchsticks or into a zig-zag shape using a serrated wave knife.

Arrange the salad ingredients on a platter and pour over the creamy turmeric dressing.

Protein and carb perfection...
A couple of handfuls of cooked quinoa or freekeh would boost the carbohydrate content of this salad, while small cubes of smoked hard cheese or shredded cooked chicken add additional protein.

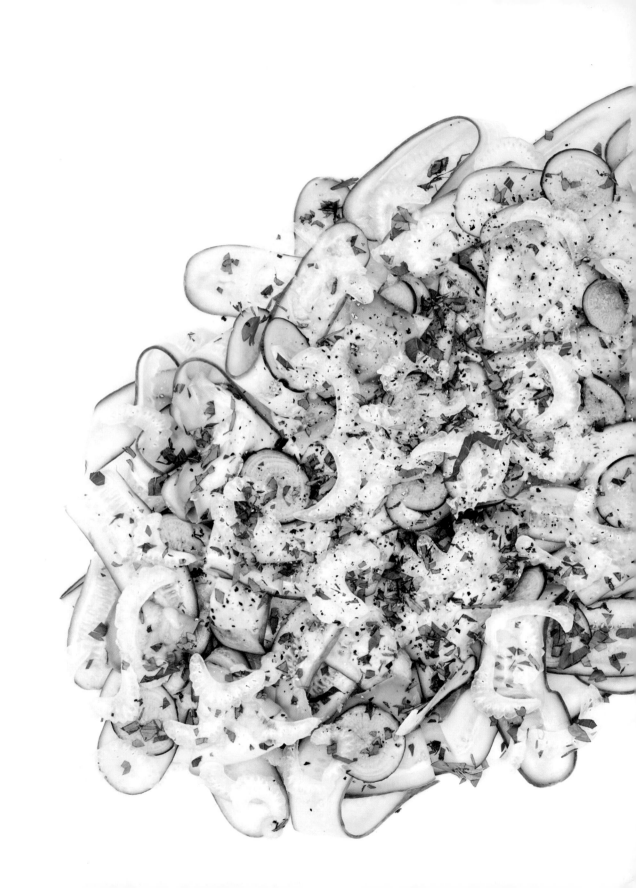

CUCUMBER 'NOODLE' SALAD WITH RAW SAFFRON CREAM

These transparent, glass-like cucumber 'noodles' are really refreshing served chilled in the summer with the Raw Saffron Cream, reminiscent of old-fashioned salad cream.

2 large cucumbers
3–4 celery sticks, trimmed
1 small raw yellow beetroot, scrubbed or peeled
1 small handful of chopped parsley or other soft-leaf herb
pepper

RAW SAFFRON CREAM
½ teaspoon powdered saffron
100g (3½oz) cashew or macadamia nuts
¼ garlic clove
1 spring onion (white part only)
½–1 teaspoon date paste or sweetener of choice
a pinch of ground paprika

The nuts in this dressing are a great source of essential fats and monounsaturates that help to lower cholesterol.

Slice the cucumbers lengthways into long, thin ribbons using a mandolin or sharp knife, and finely slice the celery and yellow beetroot. Place the vegetables on a serving platter or in a bowl.

To make the saffron cream, place all the ingredients and 150ml (5fl oz) water in a high-speed blender and blitz to a smooth, pouring consistency. Add a little extra water to thin the dressing if needed. (If you have time, you could soak the nuts for about 8 hours, or overnight, to soften them before blending.)

Spoon the saffron cream over the salad, sprinkle with the parsley and grind over some black pepper.

Perfect pairings...
This dainty salad is good with any delicately flavoured seafood such as ceviche or seared scallops, or as a refreshing addition to a Chinese or Asian-inspired meal.

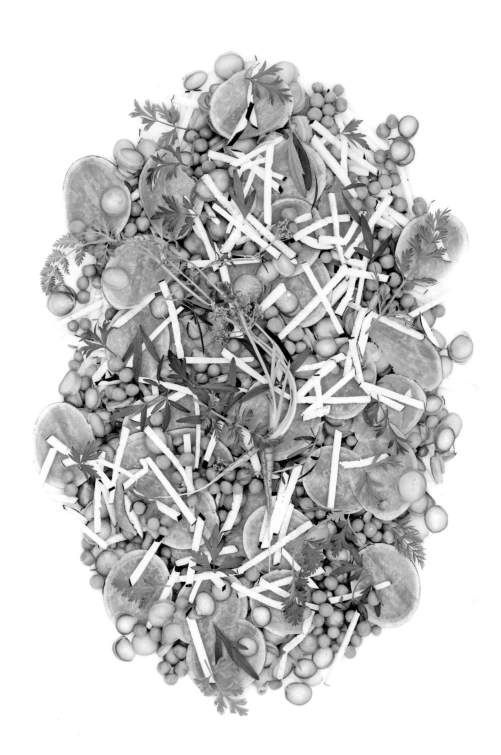

SWEET POTATO & PEA SALAD

Raw sweet potatoes are a recent find but since I've discovered how delicious they are when thinly sliced, I use them raw in salads all the time. They're quite dry in texture so absorb any dressing really well and it's good to team them up with juicier ingredients, such as the peas and asparagus in this recipe, for a contrast in colour, texture and flavour.

You could try a sweet and sour dressing, such as the Sweet Chilli & Lemon Dressing (see page 129), or the Maple, Lemon & Ginger Dressing (see page 128) with this salad.

4 large sweet potatoes
1 black radish or 4–5 regular radishes, trimmed
6–7 asparagus spears, woody ends trimmed
200g (7oz) fresh shelled or defrosted frozen peas
1 small handful of mixed chopped herbs, such as mint, chives, parsley and basil
Sweet Chilli & Lemon Dressing (see page 129) or Maple, Lemon & Ginger Dressing (see page 128)

Asparagus is a superb source of folate needed for cell division and blood formation. It's also a very important nutrient during pregnancy.

Scrub and wash the sweet potatoes well and peel if you won't want to eat the skin. Slice them into wafer-thin discs or grate coarsely.

Cut the black radish into matchsticks and slice the asparagus into small discs by cutting them across the stems.

Combine all the ingredients in a serving bowl with the dressing of your choice.

Try this...
For a light meal, serve ceviche-style with raw fish, or with sushi, or try the salad with steamed or roasted white fish.
The sweet potatoes can be cut into chips, lightly coated in coconut oil and roasted until crisp and golden before topping the salad.

SMASHED CUCUMBER SALAD

It might seem a little extreme to smash up the cucumbers, but the rough edges of the pieces soak up the Middle Eastern-style Za'atar Dressing (see page 134) really well and look unusual in this salad.

Cucumber is hydrating and very low in calories, while sesame seeds are high in anaemia-protective iron.

4 large cucumbers
Za'atar Dressing (see page 134)
3 tablespoons sesame seeds
red chillies, to garnish

To smash your cucumbers, hold one firmly by the end and gently bash with a rolling pin, being careful not to splatter the juices and pieces of cucumber everywhere. Cut any larger pieces into chunks then repeat with the rest of the cucumbers.

Place the cucumbers on a serving platter or in a bowl and pour over the za'atar dressing. It's really nice to let this salad marinate for 30 minutes or so. Mix again just before serving and scatter over the sesame seeds. Garnish with the red chillies.

For a cooked alternative...
Sear the cucumber on a hot grill until lightly charred in places.
The freshness of this dish would work well with any Middle Eastern-style meal.

CRUNCHY WINTER VEG SALAD

Raw winter root vegetables are so much easier to eat and digest when they're cut into wafer-thin slices. To bring out the aniseed-flavour of the fennel, serve this salad with the Tarragon Vinaigrette (see page 126), or scatter a few fresh tarragon leaves or fronds of bronze fennel over the salad before serving.

The pumpkin seeds are great as they are or you could try toasting them in a dry or lightly oiled frying pan for a few minutes until they are lightly browned at the edges and have popped open slightly. They have a wonderful toasted flavour and crunch. If you salt them afterwards they make a great snack, too.

2 red leaf lettuces
2–3 raw yellow or red beetroots, scrubbed or peeled
1 fennel bulb
Tarragon Vinaigrette (see page 126)
3 tablespoons pumpkin seeds
1 small handful of chopped mixed herbs, such as thyme, chives, parsley and tarragon

Pumpkin seeds are an excellent source of zinc, which is needed for cognitive function, fertility and reproduction.

Tear the lettuces into bite-sized pieces and scatter over a large serving platter.

Very finely slice the beetroot and fennel and add to the platter.

Pour over the tarragon vinaigrette and mix gently to combine and then scatter over the pumpkin seeds and chopped herbs.

Flavour favours...
Sprinkle shavings of Parmesan or crispy pancetta over the top of this salad for a flavour boost.
Try roasting the fennel until tender to give it a milder, sweeter flavour.

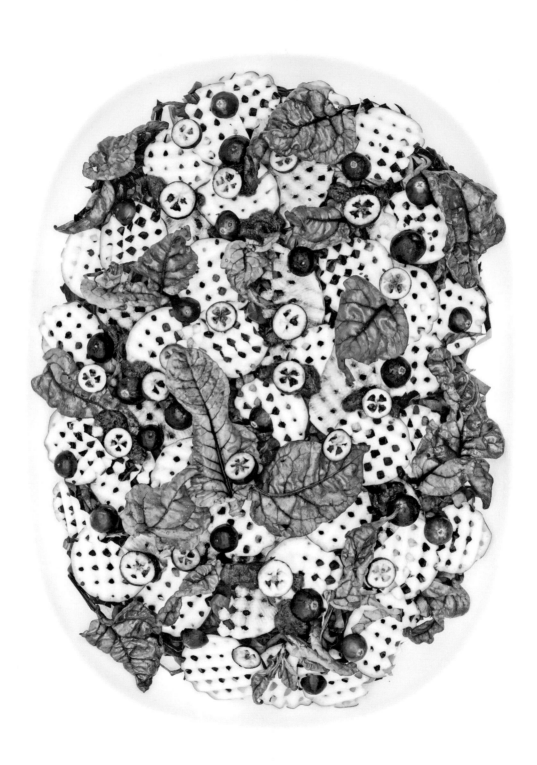

COURGETTE, CHARD & CRANBERRY SALAD

Fresh cranberries give such a festive feel to this salad, which would make a great side dish at a Thanksgiving or Christmas feast.

I've cut the courgettes into gaufrette-type (waffle or crinkle-cut) slices using a serrated wave knife – first slice the courgette one way then turn it 90 degrees and cut down to make a very thin slice, then turn it again 90 degrees to create a holey, waffle-cut slice. It takes a bit of practice to get the chequerboard effect, but it's really satisfying when you achieve it. You could also use a mandolin.

1 large bunch of baby Swiss chard
2–3 large courgettes, trimmed
300g (10½oz) fresh cranberries
3 tablespoons cranberry juice
1 teaspoon sumac
salt and pepper

You'll get plenty of potassium, vitamin A and magnesium from this salad. And cranberries are packed with antioxidants and phytochemicals that could protect against urinary infections.

Tear the leafy parts of the chard away from the stems (save the stems for juicing) and chop finely. (The leaves have been left whole in the picture for decorative effect but are best finely chopped for eating.)

Slice (see the instructions above) or grate the courgettes and mix with the chard. Set aside 200g (7oz) of the fresh cranberries to make a dressing and finely slice the rest (or leave some whole) and add to the chard and courgettes.

Place the reserved cranberries in a blender or food processor with the cranberry juice, 2 tablespoons water, sumac and seasoning and blend to a smooth consistency. You may need to add some more water or cranberry juice to thin the dressing to a pouring consistency.

When you're ready to serve the salad, pour over the dressing and mix well until it coats all of the ingredients.

A festive twist...
This also makes a great post-Christmas or post-Thanksgiving salad with added shredded roast turkey, diced roast squash and toasted sourdough croutons.

RAW MUSHROOM-TOPPED VEGETABLE SALAD

I love using raw mushrooms in salads, but I find they can be a bit too much to eat in large quantities or to have a totally 100 per cent mushroom salad.

For that reason, I'll often mix mushrooms into a salad or use them as a topping as I've done in this dish, which is great for a party. The pomegranate seeds and edible flowers add a pretty finishing touch and the finely chopped rainbow chard stems give a mild, salty taste.

This salad is photographed without a dressing but the Asian-inspired Dressing (see page 134) or Pomegranate Vinaigrette (see page 127) would both be delicious.

Mushrooms contain B complex vitamins, which help us release energy from our food, plus copper – a mineral that contributes to normal immune function.

300–400g (10½–14oz) mushrooms
3–4 stems rainbow chard
2–3 large handfuls of grated or sliced vegetables, such as pepper, carrots, raw beetroot or courgettes
1 handful of pomegranate seeds
edible flowers, to garnish
Asian-inspired Dressing (see page 134)
or Pomegranate Dressing (see page 127)

Thinly slice the mushrooms and very finely dice the stems of the rainbow chard.

Place the other grated and sliced vegetables on a large serving platter or in a bowl and scatter the sliced mushrooms over the top.

Sprinkle over the pomegranate seeds, diced rainbow chard stems and edible flowers and serve with the dressing of your choice.

For a cooked alternative…

Roast the mushrooms whole and place on top before serving, or top with shredded pulled pork and a light barbecue sauce.

GREEN-ON-GREEN SALAD

This is a simple salad of peas, asparagus, fresh herbs and fennel dressed simply in mandarin juice and a little seasoning. Asparagus is delicious raw, especially if it's super fresh, and you can cut it into beautiful dainty ribbons using just a vegetable peeler.

I used Sicilian green mandarins and their bracing sweet-sourness and almost herbal-y zest was all that the salad needed to moisten it and lift the grassy flavours. If you can't get hold of green mandarins then use oranges with a squeeze of lime.

Alternative, or additional, dressings would be a Lemony Salsa Verde (see page 133), Gremolata-style Dressing (see page 133), or the Green Juice Dressing (see page 128).

2 bunches of asparagus
1 large fennel bulb
300g (10½oz) shelled peas
finely grated zest and juice of 2–3 Sicilian green mandarins
1 small bunch of mixed chopped herbs, such as mint, basil, dill and parsley
salt and pepper

Your mum was definitely right when she told you to eat up your greens – this salad is packed with folate, and peas are rich in vitamin B1 (thiamin), needed for a healthy nervous system.

Snap the woody ends off the asparagus spears (the spears naturally yield and break in the right place when you gently bend them) and, using a vegetable peeler, cut into ribbon-like strands.

Finely slice or shave the fennel and mix with the asparagus along with the peas. Combine the vegetables in a serving bowl or platter.

Sprinkle the mandarin zest over the salad then squeeze over the juice and season. Scatter the herbs over the top before serving.

Hot extras...
Seared tuna, roasted chickpeas, cooked black beans or roasted cauliflower florets would all be great additions.

SWISS CHARD & TOMATO SALAD

Swiss chard is great raw in salads as the leaves are super nutritious and pair well with all sorts of other flavours, while the naturally salty stems can be used finely chopped or juiced to make a dressing without having to add any extra salt.

It comes with a Tomato Dressing (see page 133), which is one of my favourite go-to dressings. You could reserve half of the cherry tomatoes in the dressing to sprinkle over the top of the salad, rather than use all of them in the dressing.

2 radicchios
2 bunches of Swiss chard
Tomato Dressing (see page 133)
50g (1¾oz) pine nuts

The Swiss chard and tomato dressing combine to make this salad rich in vitamins and antioxidants. Pine nuts add a boost of magnesium – a mineral that's important for energy levels.

Finely shred the radicchio leaves and the leafy parts of the Swiss chard (you can juice the stems) and place them in a serving bowl.

Pour the tomato dressing over the salad and sprinkle with the pine nuts just before serving.

Bulk it up...
Bacon, blue cheese, grilled or barbecued meat or fish and/or a handful of crispy garlic croutons would add extra substance to this salad.

SWEET & SOUR VEGGIE 'NOODLES'

This light and lean salad is great to serve in the warmer months as it's crisp and refreshing with lots of fresh, zingy flavours. The Sweet & Sour Dressing is spicy and rich.

Sprouted seeds are widely considered to be one of nature's super-foods. You can buy them in most supermarkets but they're really easy to grow, too.

2 large carrots, scrubbed or peeled
2 courgettes, trimmed
1 large cucumber
3–4 spring onions, trimmed
1 large red chilli
½ red onion, peeled
1 large red pepper, deseeded
1 large mango
2 tablespoons sesame seeds
1 handful of chopped coriander
1 large handful of sprouted seeds or beansprouts

SWEET & SOUR DRESSING
2 tablespoons sesame oil
1 tablespoon date paste or sweetener of choice
1 teaspoon five-spice powder
2 teaspoons freshly grated ginger
1 small garlic clove, peeled
finely grated zest and juice of 1 lime
1 teaspoon nama shoyu or soy sauce (optional)
salt and pepper

The sprouted seeds are the super-food ingredient in this salad, bursting with enzymes and vital nutrients, and they're also a source of raw plant-based protein.

Slice the carrots (there's no need to peel them if they are organic), courgettes and cucumber into thin julienne strips or use a spiralizer to make vegetable 'noodles'.

Roughly chop the spring onions and finely chop the chilli and red onion. Cut the red pepper and mango into small dice.

Place all the salad ingredients in a large bowl along with the sesame seeds, coriander and sprouted seeds or beansprouts and mix gently together (it's easiest to do this with your hands).

To make the dressing, place all the ingredients into the bowl of a food processor and blend to a smooth, thick consistency. If you prefer a more runny dressing, thin it down with a little extra lime juice or a splash of water. Season to taste.

Pour the sweet and sour dressing over the salad and mix to combine.

Asian inspiration...
A great alternative to rice or traditional noodles, you could serve the veggie 'noodles' with any Chinese-style sauce instead of the Sweet & Sour Dressing. Alternatively, the flavour and texture of finely shredded barbecued or pulled pork, or chicken would go well.

TOMATO & ARTICHOKE SALAD

Although you can eat the very young tender hearts of artichokes raw, if you can find a raw version of preserved artichokes (often bottled in olive oil) then they're so much tastier and less fiddly to prepare.

I've added some dehydrated tomatoes to this salad for a rich, tomatoey taste (see how to dehydrate your own on page 140), but you can use fresh instead.

The vibrant Orange Vinaigrette (see page 127) helps to harmonize and enliven this salad.

2 red leaf lettuces
150g (5½oz) preserved artichoke hearts
Orange Vinaigrette (see page 127)
6–7 large dehydrated tomatoes, sliced (see page 140), or sliced fresh tomatoes
1 small handful of basil leaves

This salad is rich in tomato lycopene and a good source of vitamin C. Artichokes are used for maintaining liver health in traditional herbal medicine.

Tear the lettuce leaves into bite-sized pieces and place in a serving bowl or on a platter.

Chop the artichokes into rough chunks (or leave whole, if you prefer).

Pour the orange vinaigrette over the lettuce leaves, add the artichoke hearts and dehydrated or fresh tomatoes and mix gently to combine. Finally, scatter over the basil, tearing up any larger leaves as you go.

Cooked extras...
Roasted vegetables would be in keeping with the Mediterranean feel of this salad.
Try topping with fresh creamy cheese, hard-boiled eggs or poached eggs.
Diced barbecued meats also work well.

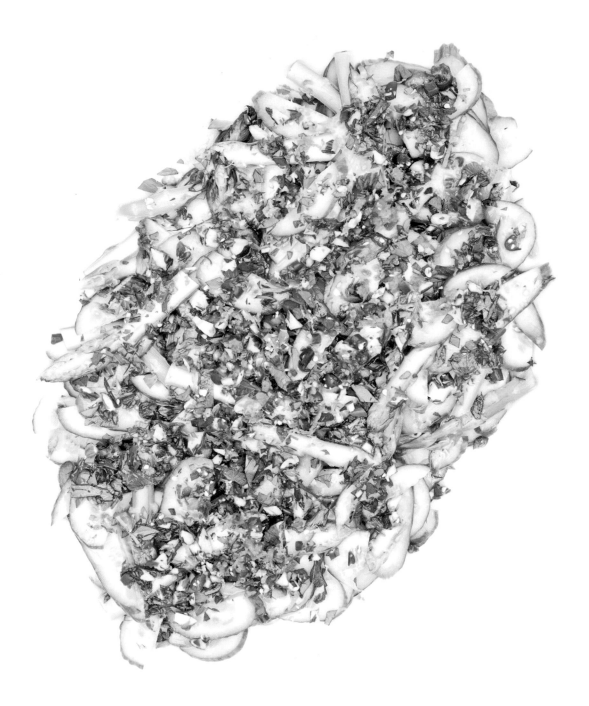

ASPARAGUS & CUCUMBER SALAD WITH SPICY ORANGE GREMOLATA

Thinly sliced asparagus and cucumber are sprinkled with a spicy orange gremolata, which adds both flavour and crunch to the vegetables.

As a gremolata is typically quite dry in texture, it's great to use with more juicy salad ingredients as the combination of the two makes the gremolata more dressing-like in consistency.

6–7 asparagus spears, woody ends trimmed
2 large cucumbers

SPICY ORANGE GREMOLATA
2 red chillies, or to taste
1 small handful of parsley leaves
150g (5½oz) almonds or walnuts
1 orange
drizzle of cold-pressed extra virgin olive oil (optional)
salt and pepper

This salad is a good source of vitamin C, folate and essential fats. Plus the chilli will give your metabolism a temporary boost.

Finely slice the asparagus and cucumbers and place in a serving bowl or on a platter.

To make the spicy orange gremolata, deseed the chillies and place them on a chopping board with the parsley leaves and almonds or walnuts. Finely grate over the orange zest and chop the whole lot together (or do this in a food processor) until you have a fine-ish, but still chunky mixture.

Sprinkle the gremolata over the cucumber and asparagus and gently mix in. Add a drizzle of olive oil, if you like, and a little seasoning.

Meat and fish...
Finely shredded Parma ham, seared tuna or peppered mackerel would all be delicious with the fresh, zingy flavours of this salad.

CARROT 'NOODLE' SALAD

Carrots are a great vegetable to spiralize as they're fairly sturdy and can be prepared and dressed well in advance so they soften slightly by the time you want to eat them. I've used orange, yellow and purple carrots and they make an attractive contrast in colours, if you can get hold of them.

Peanuts and carrots have a natural flavour affinity so I have teamed this salad with the Peanut Satay Dressing (see page 134) to echo that.

Teaming carrots with healthy fat from the peanut butter or tahini means you'll absorb more of the fat-soluble beta carotene (vitamin A) from them.

3–4 large carrots, scrubbed or peeled
1 tablespoon poppy seeds
Peanut Satay Dressing (see page 134)
edible flowers, to garnish

Spiralize the carrots (there's no need to peel them if they're organic) into 'noodles' or coarsely grate them using a box grater. Toss the carrots with the poppy seeds and arrange on a platter or place in a serving bowl.

Pour the peanut satay dressing over the carrots, toss until combined, and top with a few edible flowers.

Protein boost...
Add a few handfuls of chopped spinach, toasted nuts and seeds, or shredded barbecued meat.
The satay-type peanut dressing teams well with any kind of cooked chicken.

RADICCHIO & BRUSSELS SPROUT SALAD

I'm a sucker for a pink and green coloured salad!

The smaller inside leaves of a radicchio are often paler and more pinky in colour than the outer leaves and they look really pretty against the green of the Brussels sprouts.

Shaving the Brussels sprouts so they're wafer thin is a great way to incorporate them raw into a salad as they can often go undetected by cabbage-phobic diners if mixed in well.

This crunchy vibrant salad is great served with the Pistachio Pesto (see page 132) or Pomegranate Vinaigrette (see page 127).

2 radicchios
2 soft-leaf green lettuces
200g (7oz) Brussels sprouts
100g (3½oz) shelled pistachio nuts
Pistachio Pesto (see page 132) or
Pomegranate Vinaigrette (see page 127)
1 small handful of mixed chopped herbs, such as parsley, dill, thyme, oregano and basil

Brussels sprouts are little powerhouses of nutrition – rich in folate, vitamin C and phytochemicals that may reduce your cancer risk.

Tear the leaves of the radicchio and lettuce into bite-sized pieces.

Shave or slice the Brussels sprouts very finely and chop the pistachio nuts.

Combine all the ingredients together in a bowl and serve with the dressing of your choice and sprinkled with herbs.

For a cooked alternative...

Roast, grill or sear the radicchio on a barbecue.
The outer leaves of the Brussels sprouts could be roasted until crisp.
For an extra protein element try cooked salmon, marinated tempeh or tofu.

APPLE 'SPAGHETTI' WITH AUTUMN FRUIT

I've spiralized the apples in this light autumnal salad to make 'spaghetti' and then teamed them with black dessert grapes and golden-coloured cubes of Sharon fruit. It comes with an aromatic and vibrant orange and passion fruit sauce.

I used vine leaves in this photo to give the recipe a truly autumnal feel, but don't include these in your salad.

Red-skinned apples are a good source of polyphenol antioxidants associated with a reduced risk of cardiovascular disease.

3 large passion fruits
finely grated zest and juice of 1 orange
1 small bunch of seedless black grapes
juice of 1 lemon
3 large red-skinned apples
3 large Sharon fruit (persimmon)

To make the sauce, halve the passion fruits, scoop out the flesh and place in a bowl with the orange zest and juice. Mix everything together and chill until ready to serve.

While the sauce is chilling, de-stem and halve the grapes.

Prepare an acidulated water bath to prevent the apple discolouring. Squeeze the lemon juice into a large bowl filled with about 200ml (7fl oz) of cold water.

Make the apple 'spaghetti' using a spiralizer or julienne peeler, or cut them into matchsticks. Place the prepared apples in the water bath and gently swirl them around so all the pieces are coated, then drain well on kitchen paper. Cut the Sharon fruit into dice.

To assemble the fruit salad, pile the apple spaghetti in the middle of a large bowl and scatter over the Sharon fruit and black grapes, then pour over the orange and passion fruit sauce.

Smooth servings...
Blend the fruit with coconut water to make a delicious dairy-free smoothie.
The Sharon fruit could be grilled or seared on a barbecue to give another flavour and texture to the salad.
Serve the fruit with a drizzle of natural yogurt or cream.

VEGGIE 'NOODLES' WITH COCONUT CURRY SAUCE

Although rich, this sauce is fresh tasting and can be gently warmed before serving, as can the 'noodles': steam them, or plunge very briefly into boiling salted water and drain thoroughly, or lightly sauté in a wok or frying pan.

2 green courgettes, trimmed
2 yellow courgettes, trimmed
1 large carrot, scrubbed or peeled
200g (7oz) sugar snap peas or fresh shelled peas
2 sweetcorn cobs, outer husks removed
1 large handful of chopped mixed herbs, such as coriander, parsley, rosemary, oregano and thyme
fresh coconut shavings and lime wedges, to serve

COCONUT CURRY SAUCE
meat and milk from 1 fresh young coconut (or 200ml/ 7fl oz coconut milk, 300ml/ ½ pint coconut water and 150g/5½oz unsweetened desiccated coconut)
1 banana shallot, peeled
½ green chilli
1 teaspoon grated fresh ginger
1 small garlic clove, peeled
finely grated zest and juice of 1 lime
1 teaspoon medium-hot curry powder
2.5cm (1in) piece fresh turmeric or 2 teaspoons ··· ground turmeric
salt and pepper

The turmeric in this sauce has anti-inflammatory properties. Combining the spice with a good grating of fresh black pepper – rich in piperine – increases its bio-availability to your body.

Cut the green and yellow courgettes and carrot into long 'noodles' using a julienne peeler or spiralizer. Cut the sugar snap peas into fine diagonal shreds and slice the sweetcorn kernels away from the cobs.

To make the sauce, blend together the meat and milk of the fresh coconut (or the coconut milk, coconut water and desiccated coconut, if using) with the rest of the ingredients until creamy and silky smooth, then season to taste. (Juice the turmeric first if you are using the fresh root.)

Place all the vegetables in a large bowl, pour over the coconut curry sauce and mix well.

Leave the salad to marinate for 30 minutes until the noodles soften slightly, then sprinkle over the chopped herbs and serve with shavings of fresh coconut (or you could use desiccated coconut) and wedges of lime for squeezing over.

Meaty ideas...
A handful of cooked peeled tiger prawns, shredded cold roasted chicken or pulled pork would work well mixed into the 'noodles'.

SIMPLE CARROT SALAD

Carrots (like courgettes) can make an almost-instant salad and are a great hunger-assuager if you're ravenous when you get back home from work and need something to eat right away. I always keep a bottle of dressing in the fridge for such 'emergencies' and after quickly grating a carrot or two you have a satisfying instant snack. This salad uses orange, yellow and purple heirloom carrots, which I've mixed with a few lettuce leaves, chopped red cabbage and fresh herbs.

A carrot salad is a kind of blank canvas when it comes to dressings as it teams with almost any type of dressing – spicy, fruity, creamy or light – but my favourites are either the Orange Vinaigrette (see page 127) or Peanut Satay Dressing (see page 134) along with a topping of chopped nuts and sultanas.

If you have organic carrots with their tops still on, reserve some of the green leaves to chop and sprinkle over the salad, they're also a great source of additional nutrients.

Carrots are a fantastic source of beta carotene, which the body converts into vitamin A, needed for healthy eyes, skin and the immune system. Carrot juice is also a great way to drink up the benefits of this vegetable and the creamy-sweet juice makes a good salad dressing in itself.

4–6 large carrots, preferably heirloom, scrubbed or peeled
¼ small red cabbage
1 small lettuce of choice
1 handful of mixed chopped soft-leaf herbs,
such as parsley, dill, coriander and basil
dressing of choice

Chop, slice or grate the carrots (if they're organic there's no need to peel them) and place them in a large bowl.

Finely chop the red cabbage and tear the lettuce into bite-sized pieces. Mix the vegetables into the carrots with the herbs.

Pour your dressing of choice over the salad just before serving and enjoy.

Raw and cooked...
Try combining both raw and cooked versions of the same vegetable in a salad. Here, you could add some roasted carrots for a spectrum of carrot-on-carrot flavours and textures.

ROCKET & RADISH SALAD WITH SPIRULINA DRESSING

I've used Bangladeshi lemons in this recipe as I love their ridged and crinkled green skin and super-bracing acidity. I only come across them occasionally so a regular yellow lemon is an adequate substitute.

400g (14oz) wild rocket leaves
1 watermelon radish or 3–4 regular radishes, trimmed
3–4 okra
1 large Bangladeshi lemon or regular lemon (optional)
Spirulina Dressing (see page 135), or sprinkling of spirulina powder, or dressing of your choice

Spirulina is a blue-green algae super-food, while rocket is a super-green rich in iron, folate and vitamin A.

Scatter the rocket over a large serving platter or into a large bowl. Finely slice the radish and okra and add to the rocket.

If you have a super-sharp mandolin, you can slice the Bangladeshi lemon microscopically thin so it's palatable raw, or just use the finely grated zest and juice in the spirulina dressing and leave out the sliced lemon in the salad.

Pour the dressing over the salad or sprinkle a little of the spirulina powder on top, as I have done here, and choose a dressing of your choice.

Sides and smalls...

The peppery taste of this rocket salad would complement any raw or cooked fish dish, or it could be served in small portions as a palate cleanser between courses.

WATERMELON & SUNFLOWER SEED SALAD

A vibrant summer salad for when watermelons are at the peak of sweet and juicy ripeness and sunflowers are in full bloom.

Interestingly you can eat almost every part of a sunflower at each stage of its life cycle. The sprouted seeds are fantastic in a salad and the petals used here give a mild, nutty taste in addition to the crunch of the seeds.

I've used red-veined sorrel as its slightly sour, acidic leaves act as a balance to the sweetness of the melon, but spinach or rocket with a squeeze of lemon makes a good substitute.

Watermelon is a great and refreshing way to hydrate in hot weather as the flesh is 92 per cent water. The pink colour comes from lycopene (also in tomatoes), which has been associated with a lower risk of cardiovascular disease.

1 large watermelon
1 large handful of sorrel leaves or baby spinach leaves
200g (7oz) sunflower seeds
petals from 3–4 sunflowers
salt and pepper

Smash up your watermelon and break it into bite-sized pieces, or cut it into large chunks, reserving any juices to use as a simple dressing.

Roughly tear the sorrel or spinach leaves and mix with the watermelon in a large bowl or on a platter. Season to taste, adding some of the watermelon juices.

Scatter over the sunflower seeds and petals before serving.

For a great flavour combination...
Serve as a side salad at a barbecue with some feta crumbled over and a handful of chopped fresh mint for a great flavour combination.

DRAGON FRUIT SALAD WITH PASSION FRUIT & CLEMENTINE DRESSING

Dragon fruit look beautifully surreal with their bright pink skin and soft green spikes. I've yet to find a way of identifying if their inside flesh will be white or bright magenta pink, so every time I cut into one it's a surprise.

This tropical fruit salad with pineapple, pomelo, physalis (Chinese/cape gooseberry) and guava is dressed simply with a good squeeze of clementine juice and some passion fruit pulp. When fruit looks and tastes this good it doesn't need much else doing to it.

1 large pineapple
2 pomelo
2–3 guava
12 physalis
3 large dragon fruit
3 clementines
4 passion fruit
mint leaves, to decorate

Every 80g (3oz) serving of a different fruit counts as a portion towards your 5-a-day – meaning there are at least three portions per person in this salad.

Peel and core the pineapple and chop the flesh into chunks, then peel the pomelo and cut into segments.

Cut the guava in half and scoop out the flesh and remove the papery outside leaves from the physalis.

Remove the skin from the dragon fruit and chop into chunks or cut into shapes – I cut them into star shapes.

Arrange all the prepared fruit on a platter or place in a serving bowl. Cut the clementines in half and squeeze the juice over the fruit salad and cut the passion fruit in half and spoon over their seedy pulp. Finally scatter over a few fresh mint leaves before serving.

Skewers and smoothies...
As an alternative way to present this salad, cut the fruit into bite-sized pieces and thread onto skewers.

Blend the fruit with natural yogurt and a handful of oatmeal or raw oats as a filling breakfast smoothie.

PEPPER SALAD WITH CRUSHED TOMATO & ORANGE SALSA

The flavours of the peppers, oranges and tomatoes go really well together and they look so cheerful. By mixing the oranges with tomatoes in the salsa you get a great sweet/salty/savoury flavour combination, which is also delicious served with avocado.

4–5 red and orange peppers
1 handful of chopped mixed herbs, such as thyme, chives, parsley, basil and dill, plus extra to garnish

CRUSHED TOMATO & ORANGE SALSA
2 oranges
300g (10½oz) cherry tomatoes
3 spring onions, trimmed
a splash of cold-pressed extra virgin olive oil
salt and pepper

Peppers and oranges are two of the richest sources of vitamin C, making this a great salad for a strong immune system.

Deseed and finely slice the peppers, sprinkling them with the chopped herbs as you add them to a serving bowl.

To make the salsa, cut away the peel and pith from the oranges and segment the flesh over a bowl to catch any juices, discarding the white membrane. Roughly chop the orange segments.

Halve the tomatoes and press down gently on them to crush them and release their juices. Place the tomatoes and oranges in a bowl and scrape any remaining tomato juice from your chopping board into the bowl along with the 'captured' orange juice.

Finely chop the spring onions and add to the tomato and oranges with the olive oil and seasoning and stir gently together. The salsa is best left at room temperature for an hour or so for the flavours to develop and mingle, but it can be used straightaway.

When you're ready to serve, spoon the salsa over the herby peppers and garnish with a few extra herbs.

Try this...
Avocado – plain, grilled or baked until super creamy – is the perfect addition to this salad, or shredded roast chicken and toasted sesame seeds would be delicious, too.

RAINBOW VEGETABLE 'COUSCOUS'

A mixed vegetable 'couscous' is a great way of using up any veg you have lurking in the fridge, and it makes a healthy low-carb alternative to traditional couscous.

I've used a spectrum of different coloured fresh vegetables and blitzed them to an even-sized 'grain' to give the same texture as couscous. I tend to process the different vegetables in separate batches to keep the colours distinct and then mix them together at the last minute.

Dry-textured vegetables are best so the grains keep separate and fluffy, but if you do use juicier veg just place them on kitchen paper after blitzing to absorb any moisture before mixing with the rest of the ingredients. Depending on which veg you use, this salad can be eaten on its own or with a vinaigrette dressing mixed in.

2–3 peppers (red, orange or yellow)
1 large sweet potato, peeled
150g (5½oz) baby sweetcorn
3–4 kale leaves
2 raw red or candy beetroot, scrubbed or peeled
2 large carrots, scrubbed or peeled
½ small red cabbage
½ head broccoli
1 small bunch of radishes, trimmed

The vibrant reds, yellows and greens in this salad make it a rich source of carotenoid antioxidants that help to protect skin and keep the immune system healthy.

Prepare the vegetables as needed then chop them into rough chunks. Blitz the vegetables individually in a food processor to a fine, grainy texture. Take care not to over process them as they can become too mushy and place the peppers on kitchen paper to absorb any excess moisture.

Tip all the blitzed veg into a large bowl and mix gently together with your hands or a large spoon until everything is well combined. Serve with or without a dressing of your choice.

If you lIke it hot...
Briefly sauté the 'couscous' in a large wok or heat in a microwave. Serve instead of couscous or rice as an accompaniment, or use as the base of a salad and add protein, such as fish, chicken or meat, and a topping of your choice.

COURGETTI BOLOGNESE

'Courgetti' has the same texture of cooked pasta but is low-carb. For pappardelle-style noodles, slice the courgettes into wide ribbons instead of spiralizing. If you don't like courgettes use carrots, cucumber or butternut squash instead. This 'courgetti' is topped with a tomato-based sauce full of lovely Mediterranean flavours, and finished with a sprinkling of cauliflower 'Parmesan'. Soaked walnuts give the sauce a 'meaty' texture.

4 courgettes, trimmed
3–4 small cauliflower florets

SAUCE
50g (1¾oz) sun-dried tomatoes
4 Medjool dates
100g (3½oz) walnuts
1 carrot, scrubbed or peeled
½ raw red beetroot, scrubbed or peeled
½ red onion, peeled
1 garlic clove, peeled

½ red chilli
½ red pepper
1 celery stick, trimmed
1 small handful of parsley
1 rosemary sprig
350g (12oz) cherry tomatoes
finely grated zest and juice of 1 lemon
2 handfuls of Greek basil leaves (or use regular basil)
salt and pepper

Walnuts are a source of vitamin E and the omega-3 fat linolenic acid, which can help to maintain a healthy cholesterol level.

Start the sauce a day early. Roughly chop the sun-dried tomatoes and stone the dates. Place both in a small bowl and pour over 200ml (7fl oz) water. Place the walnuts in a bowl and pour over enough water to cover. Leave both bowls in the fridge overnight.

The next day, roughly chop the carrot, beetroot, onion and garlic. Deseed and finely chop the chilli and red pepper. Roughly chop the celery, parsley and rosemary needles. Chop 50g (1¾oz) of the cherry tomatoes into quarters and set aside.

Place the garlic, rosemary and chilli in the bowl of a food processor and blitz until finely chopped. Add the carrot, celery, red pepper and onion and blitz again.

Drain and rinse the walnuts and add to the other ingredients in the processor with the beetroot, remaining fresh tomatoes, lemon zest and juice, soaked dates and sun-dried tomatoes (including their soaking water), parsley and half the basil leaves. Process the mixture until it forms a thick sauce and the walnut pieces resemble 'minced meat' in texture. Season to taste. Depending on how juicy the tomatoes are, you may need to add a little extra water to thin the consistency of the sauce.

Spiralize the courgettes into long, curly strands or slice into long, thin strips using a julienne or vegetable peeler.

Blitz the cauliflower florets in a processor until the texture of fine grains. If it contains a lot of water, place the 'parmesan' on kitchen paper to soak up the moisture.

Scatter the courgetti over a large platter, pour over the sauce, sprinkle with the reserved chopped tomatoes, cauliflower 'parmesan' and the remaining basil leaves.

- For extra flavour...
- Scatter over freshly grated Parmesan or Pecorino Romano before serving.
- Blend a few preserved anchovies into the sauce.
- Both the 'courgetti' and the sauce can be heated up.

CARROT, FIG &
BLUEBERRY SALAD

I've left the blueberries whole in this salad, but you can blend them with a little seasoning to make a vibrantly coloured fresh dressing instead of the Herb Vinaigrette (see page 126) or Lemon Shallot Vinaigrette (see page 126).

To encourage the ribbons of carrot to curl, I've put them in a bowl of iced water overnight. This is a great way of curling any finely sliced vegetables and I often do it with spring onions and fennel as their spiky bits curl and contort into all sorts of pretty shapes.

Carrots, almonds, figs, spinach and blueberries can all legitimately be described as super-foods. As an added bonus, new research suggests almonds aren't as calorific as once thought – up to one-third of their calories pass through us unabsorbed.

3–4 large carrots, scrubbed or peeled
100g (3½oz) whole almonds
5 figs
400g (14oz) baby leaf spinach
200g (7oz) blueberries
Herb Vinaigrette (see page 126) or
Lemon Shallot Vinaigrette (see page 126)

Using a vegetable peeler, cut the carrots into thin ribbons (there is no need to peel them if they're organic) and either use them straightaway, or place in an ice bath (bowl of cold water with ice cubes) overnight. (If using this method just ensure that you drain the carrot slices very well afterwards and leave them on a piece of kitchen paper to soak up any excess water before adding them to the salad.)

When you're ready to serve the salad, chop the almonds and slice the figs.

Place the spinach leaves in a bowl. Add the carrots, blueberries, figs and almonds. Pour over the dressing of your choice before serving.

Try this...
You can roast the carrots in this salad instead of serving them raw and for additional protein, try marinated tempeh or shredded roast chicken.

MANGO, BEETROOT, KALE & RADISH SALAD

For this salad you can either chop the kale finely or break it into pieces and massage it in the mango dressing. It can get a bit messy, but tastes delicious!

I've cut the yellow beetroot and pink watermelon radishes into decorative shapes for the photograph, but slice, grate or shave them as you prefer.

If you'd like to serve a dressing with this salad then I recommend the Orange Vinaigrette (see page 127).

2 large bunches of kale
2 teaspoons cold-pressed extra virgin olive oil
3 ripe mangoes
1 large raw yellow beetroot, scrubbed or peeled
1 large watermelon radish or 5–6 regular radishes, trimmed
Orange Vinaigrette (see page 127) (optional)

Colourful vegetables tend to be the most nutritious – meaning there are loads of vitamins and antioxidants, including lycopene, lutein and vitamin C in this salad.

Tear the leafy parts of the kale away from the stems (save these for juicing) and remove any tough veins in the leaves. Tear the leaves into 2.5–5cm (1–2in) pieces and place in a large bowl.

Anoint the kale leaves in the olive oil and start to massage and scrunch them with your fingers. It will take a while for the leaves to yield but they will gradually start to soften and become more pliable and tender. They're done when they feel silky soft.

Peel and stone the mangoes. If the mangoes are really ripe it's a good idea to massage them into the kale as they may be difficult to cut up neatly. Simply mush them up with your hands and get going.

Slice, grate or shave the beetroot and watermelon radish, or cut into decorative shapes and scatter them over the salad just before serving. Pour over the orange vinaigrette, if using.

Try this...
Roast the beetroot or make crispy chips from the kale to give an additional textural element to this salad.
A handful of cooked brown rice or quinoa would make a more substantial dish.

RED FRUIT SALAD

I love making salads of single or tonal colours and this platter of predominantly red-coloured fruit showcases some of the wonderful varieties available in the summer and early autumn.

As the fruit is fairly juicy it doesn't really need a dressing, but you could squeeze over the juice of 2–3 oranges, if you like.

If you're making this salad ahead, layer the fruit in a bowl with the sturdiest ones, such as the grapes, on the bottom and the more fragile fruit, such as the redcurrants and strawberries, on the top so they don't get too squashed. Then just gently mix everything together before serving.

Fruits in the red/purple spectrum are rich in anthocyanin antioxidants that can improve the strength and flexibility of our skin and blood vessels, and have anti-inflammatory qualities.

400g (14oz) strawberries
200g (7oz) redcurrants
1 small bunch of seedless black grapes
6–8 plums
4 ripe nectarines
150g (5½oz) raspberries
200g (7oz) blackberries

Remove the green tops from the strawberries and cut in half.

De-stem some of the redcurrants, leaving some intact to decorate the top, and de-stem the grapes.

Remove the stones from the plums and nectarines and cut into thick slices or bite-sized pieces.

Arrange the fruit on a platter, decorating with the redcurrant sprigs before serving.

Smooth alternatives...
The fruits in this salad would make a delicious juice or smoothie, blended together with or without natural yogurt.
Or you could serve them as a topping for pavlova.

WATERMELON & CUCUMBER SALAD

This salad is particularly good in the summer months with the cooling, refreshing flavours and textures of watermelon and cucumber. You can score the outside of the cucumber with a lemon zester to give it a decorative effect when sliced.

The red onion in this salad is rich in quercetin, which has natural anti-inflammatory and anti-histamine qualities. One to eat in the hay fever season.

1 small watermelon
1 large cucumber
½ red onion, peeled
1 small handful of mint sprigs
2 tablespoons raw apple cider vinegar
½ teaspoon sumac
1 handful of microgreens or sprouted seeds
1 handful of cress
salt and pepper

Cut the melon in half and remove the seeds. Using a melon baller, scoop out small balls of melon or chop the flesh into chunks (reserve the juice to make a dressing).

Cut the cucumber in half lengthways and scoop out the seeds with a teaspoon, then slice into crescent shapes.

Very finely slice the red onion and pick the leaves from the mint sprigs.

To make a quick dressing, combine 3–4 tablespoons of the watermelon juice, the apple cider vinegar, sumac and a little seasoning.

Place the melon balls, cucumber slices and red onion in a bowl, pour over the dressing and, using your hands, mix gently to combine. Finally scatter over the microgreens or sprouted seeds and cress.

Perfect pairings...
The addition of chopped ripe tomatoes would work well with this dish, as would a handful of feta cheese crumbled over the top.

SNOWBERRY SALAD

This sweet salad is inspired by a dessert from the Ivy restaurant in London, where frozen berries were served with a warm white chocolate sauce.

My raw almond cream tastes chocolatey – in a white chocolate sort of way – as it's vanilla-flavoured, creamy and sweet. I make it using a high-speed blender and it's so rich and silky-smooth, you wouldn't believe it isn't dairy cream! If you don't have a powerful blender use cashew nuts instead as they're softer and blend to a smoother consistency more easily.

You may find the blending process results in a slightly warm cream that will start to thaw the berries when you pour it over. For a warmer sauce, heat it in a small basin over a pan of gently boiling water.

A final sprinkle of goji berries adds a super-food kick with a contrasting chewy texture and a little extra sweetness.

Blackberries are packed with anthocyanins that have antioxidant and anti-inflammatory properties.

1 small bunch of seedless grapes
250g (9oz) redcurrants
225g (8oz) raspberries
250g (9oz) blackberries
2 tablespoons goji berries

RAW ALMOND CREAM
200g (7oz) almonds
6 Medjool dates, pitted
1 tablespoon organic virgin coconut oil
seeds from 1 vanilla pod

It's best to start this dish a day before you need it so the berries can freeze properly but, saying that, they're also lovely served semi-frozen after a couple of hours in the freezer so choose whichever you fancy.

You can also start to make the raw almond cream by soaking the nuts overnight in water, and soaking the dates separately in 500ml (18fl oz) water.

Wash and dry the fresh fruit well and pluck the grapes from the vine and redcurrants from the stems, leaving a few intact to decorate the top.

Open freeze the fruit by spreading it out on a parchment paper-lined tray or plates and placing in the freezer. This keeps the fruit separate and undamaged.

To make the raw almond cream, drain and rinse the soaked almonds then blend with the other ingredients (including the soaking water from the dates) until smooth and creamy. Add a little more water if the cream looks too thick.

Tip the frozen berries on to a platter or into a large bowl (being careful not to handle them too much to disturb their frosted coating), then drizzle over the almond cream and sprinkle with the goji berries.

Smooth and cool alternatives...
Turn this salad into a fruit-filled smoothie with a little water or coconut water, or freeze into ice pops.

CONFETTI FRUIT PLATTER WITH AN ORANGE & MANGO DRESSING

This is not a recipe as such, more a suggestion of how to present a wonderful platter of fruity ingredients. I love to serve fruit on a big communal platter as then people can pick the bits they want to eat.

I've used different cutting techniques and tools to create the various shapes and effects: two different sizes of melon baller (a standard and a mini 5mm, ¼in, one) were used to make the melon and papaya balls, and an ice cream scoop to shape the large melon curls. Then I've cut the kiwi fruit into zig-zag halves by making a serrated cut around the equator of the fruit and pulling the two halves apart. The Sharon fruit are simply chopped into dice, while the plums are sliced.

The platter is finished with a sprinkling of yellow rose petals and finely chopped fuchsias.

The combination of orange and mango makes a beautiful bright orange dressing and this silky-smooth sauce is almost like a fresh fruit custard. It's lovely poured over chopped fresh fruit, or try it with the Apple 'Spaghetti' with Autumn Fruit (see page 92).

This fruity bonanza isn't just delicious – a serving will also provide around 4 of your 5-a-day!

2 large white Asian pears
2 cantaloupe melons
1 pomegranate
1 papaya
1 Sharon fruit (persimmon)
3 plums
3–4 kiwi fruit
2 nectarines
1 handful of edible flowers, to decorate

ORANGE & MANGO DRESSING
2 ripe mangoes
finely grated zest and juice of 1 large orange
3 Medjool dates, pitted
2 tablespoons coconut water

Slice, dice, scoop and prepare your fruit as you wish, then arrange them artistically on a platter.

For the dressing, peel, stone and dice the mangoes. Add to a blender with the rest of the ingredients and process until silky smooth.

Scatter over a few edible flowers as a finishing touch – beautiful!

Smooth and cool alternatives...
Blend the fruit for an exotic-tasting smoothie, or freeze the blended fruit to make a sorbet or granita.

SCARLET SLAW

This festive slaw is made with winter fruit and vegetables and served with a Citrus & Beetroot Dressing (see page 128), which turns the salad a gorgeous shade of scarlet. The salad keeps really well in the fridge for up to 4–5 days and is even better for doing so as the flavours get a chance to mingle and develop.

This slaw is packed with cruciferous veg, antioxidant-rich cranberries and blood pressure-lowering beetroot.

½ Savoy cabbage
250g (9oz) Brussels sprouts
1 handful of flat leaf parsley
6–8 kumquats
1 red onion, peeled
3 small carrots, scrubbed or peeled
2 large Braeburn apples
juice of 1 lemon
1 handful of dried cranberries
Citrus & Beetroot Dressing (see page 128)

Finely shred the cabbage and Brussels sprouts by either cutting them very, very finely or using the shredding disc on a food processor.

Roughly chop the parsley and finely slice the kumquats and red onion. Slice the carrots crossways into thin discs (there's no need to peel them if they are organic).

Cut the apples into matchsticks then toss them in the lemon juice to stop them discolouring.

To assemble the salad, gently toss all the ingredients together, including the cranberries, in a large bowl. Pour over the citrus and beetroot dressing and mix gently again. If you keep it for a few days covered in the fridge, mix again before serving to combine.

With some cheese, please...
The sweetness of the cranberries, apples and citrus in this salad are complemented perfectly by a salty tasting cheese like feta, or a creamy goats' cheese.

PASSION FRUIT SLAW

This salad is full of fresh, crisp natural goodness, while the Passion Fruit Dressing (see page 128) lends a tropical sweetness. The longer you leave the salad to marinate in the dressing, the softer and more pliable the shredded raw vegetables will become.

1 sweetheart cabbage
2 celery sticks, trimmed
3 large asparagus spears, woody ends removed
3 spring onions, trimmed
1 carrot, scrubbed or peeled
1 large green apple
Passion Fruit Dressing (see page 128)
salt and pepper
extra passion fruit pulp and finely
shredded spring onions, to serve

This dish is high in fibre and vitamin C – an important immune system nutrient all year round, but especially during the cold and flu season!

Finely slice the cabbage, celery, asparagus and spring onions and grate the carrot and apple, discarding the core. Toss the ingredients together in a large bowl.

Pour the passion fruit dressing over the salad, mix well and season to taste. Eat straightaway or cover and refrigerate for 1–2 days to let the slaw soften slightly and to allow the flavours to meld and develop.

Mix well before serving and spoon over a little extra passion fruit pulp and top with a few finely shredded spring onions.

For a super side...
Serve as a side salad to grilled or roasted meats, or as an accompaniment to a cottage cheese-stuffed jacket potato.

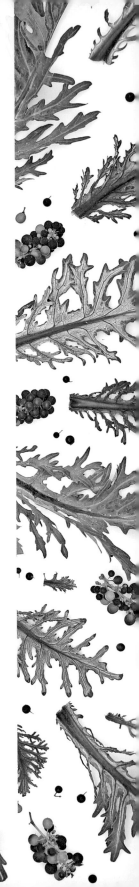

KALE SLAW

When I was a young, kale was often grown as cattle feed but now not many people need convincing of the 'super-powers' of the mighty kale! My favourite variety is cavolo nero (dino kale), which is great juiced, blended into a smoothie or massaged into silky submission in a salad. But I can never resist the more decorative types of kale too – the pink, purple, white and frilly-edged varieties sometimes look so unreal.

In this slaw, I've shredded the leaves and very finely chopped the tender parts of the stems before mixing them with a handful of grapes.

The ingredients are robust enough to handle almost any favourite dressing but I like to use the Grilled Citrus Dressing (see page 129), Pomegranate Vinaigrette (see page 127), or Creamy Green Dressing (see page 131).

Kale is absolutely packed with an antioxidant called lutein, which protects the back of the eye from UV damage. Studies suggest eating it regularly could protect against age-related macular degeneration.

1 big bunch of kale of choice, such as cavolo nero
2 large handfuls of seedless black grapes
Grilled Citrus Dressing (see page 129), Pomegranate Vinaigrette (see page 127), or Creamy Green Dressing (see page 131)

Tear the leaves away from the stems of the kale and very finely chop or thinly slice them (a chiffonade-type cut works well on any large or broad kale leaves).

To prepare the kale stems, break the tender parts away from the hard, woodier bits (reserving these for juicing) and very, very, finely chop the tender stems.

Combine the kale leaves and stems with the grapes in a large bowl and add the dressing of your choice.

Super sides and sweet sippers...
A great side dish to barbecued meats or fish.
Try juicing the kale and grapes together (the sweetness of the grapes curbs any bitterness in the kale), for a 'salad' drink.

PAPAYA SLAW SALAD

This fruity coleslaw is made with two types of cabbage to add different textures, as well as papaya, nectarines, parsley and spring onions. For extra crunch with good staying power (it doesn't go soggy), add a couple of handfuls of beansprouts.

This salad travels well so it makes good picnic fare, or if you want to make it in advance to serve at a barbecue or buffet. The juices from the fruit make their own kind of dressing, but if you want to add a traditional creamy slaw-type dressing then the Herby Ranch Dressing (see page 131) or Raw Cashew Mayo (see page 131) are both suitable.

1 Savoy cabbage
1–2 small sweetheart cabbages
1 handful of flat leaf parsley
3–4 spring onions, trimmed
1 large papaya
2–3 ripe nectarines
a pinch of dried chilli flakes (optional)
salt and pepper

This salad will give you a boost of vitamin C (papayas contain more than oranges). Savoy cabbage supplies bone-friendly calcium, too.

Finely shred both types of cabbage and finely chop the parsley and spring onions, then put everything in a large bowl.

Halve, peel and deseed the papaya and remove the stones from the nectarines. Chop both fruit into small dice and add to the bowl with the rest of the ingredients, saving any juices from the fruit to make a simple dressing.

Combine all the ingredients in the bowl with the chilli flakes and reserved juices and season to taste. Chill for 30 minutes before serving to allow the cabbage to soften and the flavours to develop.

•
•
•

Try this...
Barbecued meats, chicken or chargrilled vegetables would all make great additions to this salad as would blue cheese, crumbled over the top.

dressings

SALAD DRESSINGS

Homemade salad dressings taste so much better than shop-bought ones – not only do you know exactly what's in them, you can tweak the ingredients to suit the flavours of the salad you're making.

Dressings don't have to be complicated... sometimes a drizzle of good cold-pressed extra virgin olive oil or a simple squeeze of lemon or lime juice is all that you need. For more elaborate salads, a luxurious multi-flavoured emulsion or brightly coloured dressing is the way to take a bowl of leafy goodness to another level. A dressing can act like a 'gravy', unifying the different flavours and textural elements of your salad to give it cohesiveness.

Depending on how you're using them, dressings can be served at any temperature – hot, warm, room temperature, cold or even iced – and any recipe for a sauce, salsa or dip can be thinned down and turned into a great dressing. You can make dressings with very simple or complex flavour combinations and also have fun with

colour. Fresh turmeric makes a beautiful, vivid yellow dressing, spirulina a vibrant electric green, beetroot adds bright magenta tones, and blackberries and blueberries make a wonderfully sinister, dark-coloured dressing.

Also experiment with different flavourings – fresh, light, spicy, acidic, creamy or rich – and unusual combinations, such as the Spirulina Dressing on page 135 or my quirky suggestion for Coffee Vinaigrette (see page 127), which gives an interesting bitter note and works brilliantly with robustly flavoured greens, roasted vegetables or anything with chillies. Use a dressing to enhance the other ingredients in your salad, to counterbalance or add contrast.

It's also great to vary the texture of your dressings (smooth vs chunky) and the consistency (thick vs thin), depending on the kind of salad your dressing is going with (robust leaves/chunky cut vs delicate leaves/finely cut). So do bear in mind the prevalent textures and flavours of your salad and dress accordingly. I also sometimes like to double-dress a salad – first coating the leaves in

a light vinaigrette and then adding a second heavier, more robustly flavoured dressing. It may sound a bit OTT but it's a good way to add depth of flavour and interest to a simple bowl of leaves.

TO DRESS OR NOT TO DRESS?

To serve your salad dressed or undressed with a dressing on the side, is often a matter of personal preference, practicality and timing.

Some salads benefit from pre-dressing, such as coleslaws or ones made with starchy vegetables like carrots, sweet potatoes and squash, whereas soft leafy salads wilt quickly in a dressing so should be dressed just before serving. Other salads that contain 'juicy' ingredients, such as fruit, may not need a dressing at all. Ultimately, go with your personal preference and experiment with different ideas.

MAKING A BASIC VINAIGRETTE

My go-to dressing is always a vinaigrette. I use a basic recipe and just add to it depending on what I have to hand, what I fancy flavour-wise, and the type of salad I'm making. I usually use a 3:1 ratio of oil to acid, but may go with 1:1 to keep the fat content lower (it seems to emulsify just as well). For my base recipe, see the Mothership Vinaigrette on page 126.

A vinaigrette dressing starts with an oil element and an acid element. These are the ones I most frequently use in my dressings:

❋ **Acid:** vinegar (usually raw apple cider vinegar or balsamic vinegar), citrus juice, or other fruit and vegetable juices including beetroot, tomato or celery.

❋ **Oil:** cold-pressed extra virgin olive oil, coconut oil, flaxseed oil, flavoured oils such as lemon oil, avocado oil, chilli oil, sesame seed oil or walnut oil, and oil from bottled preserved fruit and veg such as sun-dried tomatoes or roasted peppers.

FLAVOURING A DRESSING

When I've made my base Mothership Vinaigrette (see page 126), I then add ingredients to create the flavour profile I'm looking for, and that will best suit the salad I'm making. These may be:

❋ **Sweet:** date paste or other sweeteners (stevia, agave syrup, honey, maple syrup, coconut sugar), pomegranate molasses, balsamic vinegar, chutney/jam, coconut sugar, fruit, caramelized onions, sun-dried tomatoes, fresh fruit and berries, dried fruit or sweet pickles.

❋ **Salty:** sea salt, flavoured salts, soy sauce or the equivalent, such as nama shoyu, coconut aminos or tamari, salty veg such as celery, tomatoes, Swiss chard stems or seaweed (fresh or dried).

❋ **Sour:** citrus juice such as lemon, lime or orange, lemon grass, rhubarb, yogurt, extra vinegar, fermented foods such as kimchi, kombucha, water kefir, sauerkraut or buttermilk.

❋ **Spicy/piquant:** mustard, chilli, ginger, garlic, harissa, horseradish or wasabi.

❋ **Bitter:** coffee, cacao, grapefruit juice, yuzu juice or beer.

❋ **Umami:** sun-dried tomatoes, Parmesan, seaweed (fresh or dried), miso, cured meats, anchovy or dried porcini mushrooms.

You can then use my flavour suggestions, above, to balance and enhance the taste of your dressing, remembering that:

❋ **Salty and umami flavours:** balance bitterness and enhance sweetness.

❋ **Sour flavours:** balance spice and sweetness, and enhance saltiness.

❋ **Sweet flavours:** balance sour and bitterness, and enhance saltiness.

❋ **Bitter flavours:** balance sweetness and saltiness.

❋ **Spicy flavours:** balance sour and sweet.

So, for example, if you have a salad made up of predominantly bitter radicchio or slightly spicy rocket leaves, choose a dressing with a little sweetness. Or if you have a sweet-tasting, fruit-based salad choose a dressing with a little sourness or salt... think ripe watermelon dressed with lime juice and a little salt – flavour-balanced perfection!

MIXING A DRESSING

There are various ways to mix a dressing. If it's a basic vinaigrette, I usually just whisk everything together in a jug. Other types of dressings may benefit from a different method of mixing:

❋ shake together in a screw-top jar

❋ combine in a food processor or blender (oil-based dressings emulsify best this way when the oil is trickled in slowly)

❋ grind in a pestle and mortar (or smash for chunkier dressings)

❋ juice (for thin, pure vegetable- or fruit-based dressings)

❋ add individual dressing ingredients, one-by-one, to the salad in the bowl to be mixed together before serving

❋ chop together on a board (for a chunky dressing)

Bear in mind that you'll get a different texture depending on whether you use a blender or a food processor. The latter slices and chops the ingredients so you get a rougher texture, whereas a blender breaks them down into a smooth or smooth-ish sauce depending on how long you blend them for.

Another one-bowl method is to make the dressing in the salad bowl then take your serving utensils, cross them in the bowl and pile your salad leaves on top until ready to serve. The utensils will suspend the leaves above the dressing, keeping them crisp until it's time to toss everything together.

WAYS TO APPLY A DRESSING

There are several ways to dress a salad and I find the best way for most leafy mixed salads is to simply use your hands to gently mix or toss them in the dressing, that way you can feel when everything is evenly coated. Other types of salad benefit from different methods, including:

✳ drizzle it over the top

✳ massage it into the leaves (particularly good with thick leaves such as kale)

✳ dollop it on top, like splodges of paint (good if it's a thick, heavy dressing)

✳ spray it over the salad using a fine misting bottle or spray

✳ squirt it from a plastic bottle, Jackson Pollock-style!

✳ pre-dress your salad before serving (particularly good for slaws)

✳ drizzle it over in layers, interspersing it with the salad ingredients

✳ serve it molecular gastronomy-style with 'caviar pearls' containing the dressing, so when you bite into the salad the pearl gently bursts, releasing the dressing

✳ freeze it, granita-style, then shave the iced dressing over the top of the salad

DRESSING TIPS

✳ Most homemade dressings will keep for up to 1 week stored in an airtight jar in the fridge. I also freeze dressings in small zip-lock bags or ice-cube trays with great success.

✳ I like to keep a jar of dressing in the fridge so I can knock up something to eat in minutes – simply pour the dressing over pre-prepared leaves or a pile of grated carrots or courgettes, for instance, and you have a nutritious, almost-instant, hunger assuager.

✳ If you have a slow juicer, try juicing a whole unwaxed, organic lemon – it gives a dressing the most amazing citrusy flavour.

✳ If using citrus juice in a dressing, don't waste the zest (if organic and unwaxed) as it has so much flavour. Finely grate the zest and freeze it if you don't have any immediate use for it.

✳ A peeled garlic clove placed in a jar of dressing for a few hours (or up to 1 week in the fridge) will give a lovely subtle flavour.

✳ Give your vinaigrette a different texture: try whisking it with an aerolatte milk frother to create a hollandaise-type dressing.

✳ Finally don't forget to season your dressing and adjust the flavour profile to suit the ingredients you're dressing.

Oil

Acid

Salty

Unami/Savoury

Extra flavourings

Bitter

Sweet

MOTHERSHIP VINAIGRETTE

This is my base vinaigrette recipe. I usually use a 3:1 ratio of oil to acid, unless I'm cutting back on fat and then I'll use a 1:1 ratio, or no oil at all, then blitz it in a food processor as it helps to emulsify the dressing.

2 tablespoons orange, lemon or pink grapefruit
juice, or raw apple cider vinegar, or balsamic vinegar
1 tablespoon finely grated citrus zest
1–2 teaspoons honey or maple syrup,
or 2 pitted Medjool dates (soaked until soft),
or sweetener of choice
1–2 teaspoons wholegrain mustard
1 small handful of mixed herbs, such as parsley,
mint, thyme, marjoram, chives, basil, tarragon
and dill (or you could use individual herbs rather
than a mixture)
6 tablespoons cold-pressed extra virgin olive oil
salt and pepper

Blitz all the ingredients, except the olive oil, together in a food processor.

Gradually trickle in the olive oil through the funnel while the motor is still running. After a minute or two the dressing should have emulsified and thickened, then taste and add seasoning. Store the dressing in an airtight jar in the fridge for up to 1–2 weeks.

VARIATIONS

✳ Tarragon Vinaigrette: instead of using a combination of herbs add 2 tablespoons chopped tarragon and combine with the rest of the ingredients in the Mothership vinaigrette.

✳ Herb Vinaigrette: instead of using a combination of herbs add 2 tablespoons of a combination of chopped herbs of your choice and combine with the rest of the ingredients, above.

✳ Cherry Vinaigrette: instead of the mixed herbs use 150g (5½oz) fresh de-stoned cherries with the rest of the ingredients, above.

✳ Lemon Shallot Vinaigrette: use 2–3 tablespoons lemon juice, 1 tablespoon finely grated lemon zest and 1 finely chopped shallot with the rest of the ingredients, above.

Top to bottom:
Pomegranate Vinaigrette, Coffee Vinaigrette, Sweet Smoky Paprika Vinaigrette.

POMEGRANATE VINAIGRETTE

This sweet-sour dressing is perfect with more robust salads such as the Kale Slaw (see page 120), the Radicchio & Brussels Sprout Salad (see page 91), or the Raw Mushroom-topped Vegetable Salad (see page 79).

1 tablespoon pomegranate molasses
or 3 tablespoons pomegranate juice
1 tablespoon red wine vinegar
2 tablespoons cold-pressed extra virgin olive oil
1 teaspoon date paste or sweetener of choice
2 tablespoons pomegranate seeds
salt and pepper

Blend together all the ingredients, except the pomegranate seeds, until smooth. Stir in the pomegranate seeds and season just before serving.

COFFEE VINAIGRETTE

This quirky vinaigrette works brilliantly with robustly flavoured greens or roasted vegetables, or with any salads including walnuts, chillies or beef.

1 teaspoon espresso powder or ground espresso
2 tablespoons cold-pressed extra virgin olive oil
2 teaspoons red wine vinegar
1 teaspoon date paste or sweetener of choice
salt and pepper

Whisk together all the ingredients until the espresso powder dissolves, or if you're using ground espresso let the dressing sit for at least 30 minutes, or overnight, to allow the flavours to develop. Strain the dressing, discarding the coffee grounds, and season before serving. Garnish with whole coffee beans, if you wish.

ORANGE VINAIGRETTE

This zesty, vibrant dressing enlivens the Tomato & Artichoke salad (see page 85). For a more subtle hint of garlic, place the whole clove in the dressing for 10–20 minutes, rather than grating it.

2 tablespoons cold-pressed extra virgin olive oil
finely grated zest and juice of 1 orange
1 small garlic clove, peeled
salt and pepper

Whisk together the olive oil, orange zest and juice and some seasoning, then finely grate in the garlic.

SWEET SMOKY PAPRIKA VINAIGRETTE

Smoked paprika lends a real depth of flavour to this dressing. You could serve it with the Frisée & Fig Salad (see page 67) or any carrot-based salad. And it's lovely with couscous, quinoa or roasted vegetables too.

1 shallot, peeled
1 small rosemary sprig
2 tablespoons cold-pressed extra virgin olive oil (or oil from a jar of roasted peppers)
1 tablespoon red wine vinegar
1 teaspoon sweet smoked paprika
a pinch of dried chilli flakes
salt

Finely chop the shallot and the needles from the rosemary sprig, then whisk together with the rest of the ingredients until combined. Season to taste.

CRISPY SMOKY BACON DRESSING

This is one of the dressings I use to tempt any professed 'salad-hater' and if you add the crumbled bacon or pancetta just before serving it will remain crispy for longer. Also, if you're 'double dressing' a salad, it makes an indulgent pairing with a blue cheese dressing. Try it as an alternative dressing to the Rainbow Chard & Black Radish Salad (see page 61).

4–5 thinly sliced streaky bacon rashers
or pancetta slices
1 large shallot, peeled
1 small garlic clove, peeled
2 teaspoons raw apple cider vinegar
$\frac{1}{2}$ tsp wholegrain or Dijon mustard
1 teaspoon date syrup or sweetener of choice
2 tablespoons cold-pressed extra virgin olive oil

Cook the bacon or pancetta in a dry, non-stick frying pan until golden and crispy then remove from the pan, drain on kitchen paper and allow to cool.
Finely chop the shallot and garlic, add to the pan and gently sauté in the residual bacon fat until softened and lightly browned. Remove from the heat and tip into a bowl.
Add the vinegar, mustard and date paste to the bowl and whisk until combined, slowly trickling in the olive oil at the same time so the dressing emulsifies. Finally, crumble in the bacon or pancetta just before serving.

CITRUS GINGER DRESSING

Adding fresh ginger to a dressing gives it a warm, spicy flavour, and when combined with citrus it makes a great winter-cold buster. Team this dressing with the Fig & Pomegranate Salad (see page 29).

2 large carrots, scrubbed or peeled
1cm (½in) piece fresh root ginger, peeled
1 small shallot, peeled
juice of 1 lime
salt and pepper

Put the carrots, ginger and shallot in a high-speed blender with the lime juice and 2 tablespoons water and process until smooth and creamy. Season to taste.

PASSION FRUIT DRESSING

This dressing gives a tropical sweetness and crunch to salads. It's especially good with the Passion Fruit Slaw (see page 119).

3 passion fruits
finely grated zest and juice of 1 large orange
2 tablespoons cold-pressed extra virgin olive oil
1 tablespoon poppy seeds
salt and pepper

Spoon the pulp from the passion fruits into a bowl. Whisk together the orange zest, juice and olive oil, then stir into the passion fruit pulp with the poppy seeds. Season to taste.

CITRUS & BEETROOT DRESSING

I love this earthy, fruity, vibrant dressing on the Scarlet Slaw (see page 118) as well as the Frisée & Fig Salad (see page 67).

1 large raw beetroot, scrubbed or peeled
4–5 clementines, peeled
finely grated zest of 1 lemon
salt and pepper

Juice the beetroot and clementines
and combine with the lemon zest and
a little seasoning.
(If you don't have a juicer, you could coarsely
grate the beetroot and stir it into your salad –
the colour will gradually bleed beautifully
into the other ingredients to give the same effect.
Then simply squeeze the clementine juice over
the salad and sprinkle with the lemon zest
and seasoning.)

MAPLE, LEMON & GINGER DRESSING

The slight sweetness of this dressing goes really well with bitter leaves or more robust creations, such as the Sweet Potato & Pea Salad (see page 73).

2 Meyer lemons, juiced whole, or 1 regular unwaxed
lemon mixed with 1 unwaxed mandarin/clementine
3 small shallots, peeled
1 heaped teaspoon wholegrain mustard
1–2 teaspoons maple syrup or sweetener of choice
1cm (½in) piece fresh root ginger, peeled
1–2 tablespoons cold-pressed extra virgin olive oil
a pinch of dried chilli flakes
salt and pepper

Blend all the ingredients together in a food processor until thick and emulsified. Season to taste.

GREEN JUICE DRESSING

Freshly made green juice is a wonderful oil-free dressing. Leave out the garlic if you don't like it raw or substitute chives, spring onion or shallot for a milder oniony flavour. In keeping with the green theme, serve it with the Green-on-Green Salad (see page 81).

1 large cucumber
1 small bunch of parsley, basil or coriander
1 handful of dark leafy greens, such as kale, spinach
or Swiss chard
1 Romaine or 2–3 Little Gem lettuces
2.5cm (1in) piece fresh root ginger, peeled
juice of 1 lemon
½ garlic clove, peeled
salt and pepper

Put all the ingredients through a juicer, or blend in a food processor with 100ml (3½fl oz) of water. (If blending, strain the juice through a sieve before serving.) Season and use within 30 minutes of making for maximum nutritional benefit.

Left to right: Grilled Citrus Dressing,
Roasted Red Pepper Dressing,
Citrus & Beetroot Dressing,
Passion Fruit Dressing,
Green Juice Dressing.

ROASTED RED PEPPER DRESSING

Peppers take on a wonderful rich, smoky, sweetness after roasting and when blitzed with garlic, basil and lemon, they make a magical dressing that works with meat, fish and fresh or cooked veg. Try this with the Little Gem 'Tacos' (see page 49) instead of the avocado and pepper salsa, or with the Edamame Bean Salad (see page 57).

4–5 large roasted red or orange peppers (or use ones from a jar)
1 small garlic clove, peeled
1 small handful of basil leaves
juice of 1 lemon
salt and pepper

Blend together all the ingredients in a food processor or blender until smooth and creamy. Season to taste.

ROSE HARISSA DRESSING

Rose harissa has a beautiful flavour of sweet smoky chilli, spices and rose petals, and this dressing is wonderful poured over salads and soups, or any couscous, quinoa, rice or pasta dish. Use instead of the dressing in the Sweet & Sour Veggie 'Noodles' (see page 84) or on the Raw Mushroom-topped Vegetable Salad (see page 79).

1 tablespoon rose harissa paste
2 tablespoons cold-pressed extra virgin olive oil
1 tablespoon red wine vinegar
1 teaspoon maple syrup or sweetener of choice
salt and pepper

Whisk together all the ingredients and season to taste.

SWEET CHILLI & LEMON DRESSING

This super-quick, simple dressing gives a sweet, spicy, sour note to salads. Serve it with the Green-on-Green Salad (see page 81) or Cauli-flower Salad (see page 45). For an extra spicy kick, add in one finely chopped fresh red chilli

1 spring onion, trimmed
2 tablespoons sweet chilli sauce or chilli pepper jelly
1 tablespoon lemon juice or raw apple cider vinegar
2 tablespoons cold-pressed extra virgin olive oil
salt and pepper

Finely chop the spring onion and whisk together with the rest of the ingredients. Season to taste.

GRILLED CITRUS DRESSING

Citrus fruit takes on a wonderful flavour when roasted or grilled, especially on a barbecue, as the juices become sweeter and give the dressing a delicate smoky taste. This dressing is also delicious with a few cloves of crushed roasted garlic whisked in. Try it poured over the Avocado 'Truffle' Salad (see page 27) or the Kale Slaw (see page 120).

2 large oranges, halved
2 lemons, halved
125ml (4fl oz) cold-pressed extra virgin olive oil
1 teaspoon Dijon or wholegrain mustard
1 teaspoon maple syrup or sweetener of choice
salt and pepper

Place the citrus fruit cut side down on the bars of a hot barbecue grill, or cut side up on a baking sheet under a hot grill, until they start to brown and caramelize. Remove from the heat. When cool enough to handle, squeeze the juice and flesh into a bowl. Add the rest of the ingredients and whisk to form an emulsified dressing. Season to taste.

SUN-DRIED TOMATO DRESSING

Sun-dried tomatoes add a great depth of savoury, umami flavour. They add a rich tomatoey taste to the Avocado, Tomato & Lettuce Salad (see page 38), and their sweetness combines well with the natural saltiness of the Bok Choy & Samphire Salad (see page 28).

100g (3½oz) sun-dried tomatoes preserved in oil
3 tablespoons cold-pressed extra virgin olive oil (or oil from the jar of sun-dried tomatoes)
1 teaspoon wholegrain mustard
1 teaspoon date paste or sweetener of choice
2 tablespoons light balsamic vinegar
1 teaspoon sweet smoked paprika
salt and pepper

Blend together all the ingredients in a food processor until combined but still slightly chunky. Season to taste.

BEETROOT & GOATS' CHEESE DRESSING

The earthy sweetness of the beetroot pairs well with the salty sourness of the goats' cheese, and when combined they make a super tasty and pretty pink dip-cum-dressing. As a dressing, try it with the Edamame Bean Salad (see page 57) or the Swiss Chard & Tomato Salad (see page 83) instead of the tomato dressing.

3–4 large raw beetroots, scrubbed or peeled
150g (5½oz) goats' cheese
1 garlic clove, peeled
finely grated zest and juice of 1 lemon
a pinch of ras-el-hanout
1 small handful of mixed herbs, such as dill, oregano and thyme
salt and pepper

Cut the beetroots into large chunks and cook them (roast, steam or barbecue) as you prefer until tender.

Add the beetroots to the bowl of a food processor with the other ingredients and 2–3 tablespoons water and process until you have a dressing consistency. Thin down with extra lemon juice or water, if needed, and season to taste.

CREAMY GREEN DRESSING

This is a light but fresh-tasting dressing that's lovely poured over any bowl of cooked vegetables or greens, and salads containing eggs, fish or chicken. Try it with the Cucumber 'Noodle' Salad (see page 71) instead of the Raw Saffron Cream, or with the Kale Slaw (see page 120).

1 small bunch of watercress or rocket leaves
2 tablespoons mayonnaise
2 tablespoons natural yogurt or soured cream
2 anchovy fillets
finely grated zest and juice of 1 lemon
1 small handful of mixed herbs, such as chives, dill, parsley and basil
salt and pepper

Place all the ingredients in a blender and process to a silky-smooth sauce. Season to taste.

HERBY RANCH DRESSING

This dairy-free, rich, creamy, herby, mayo-type dressing teams well with the Kale Slaw (see page 120), Simple Carrot Salad (see page 95) or Crunchy Carrot & Beetroot Salad (see page 53) instead of the Raw Cashew Mayo.

200g (7oz) cashew nuts
finely grated zest and juice of 1 large lemon
1 spring onion (white part only)
1 teaspoon date paste or sweetener of choice
a pinch of cayenne pepper
2 teaspoons walnut oil
1 small handful of chopped mixed herbs, such as chives, parsley, dill, basil and coriander
salt and pepper

Soak the cashew nuts for about 8 hours, or overnight, until softened. This will make them easier to blend to a creamy consistency.
Drain the cashews and add to a high-speed blender with the lemon zest and juice, the white part of the spring onion, the date paste, cayenne pepper, walnut oil and 250ml (9fl oz) water, then blend until smooth and creamy.
Add more water to the dressing if you prefer a thinner consistency, stir in the chopped herbs and season to taste.

RAW CASHEW MAYO

Rich and creamy, this raw cashew mayonnaise is perfect on thinly sliced crisp fresh vegetables such as the Crunchy Carrot & Beetroot Salad (see page 53) or the Waldorf Salad (see page 39). It can be flavoured with fresh herbs, mustard, a touch of garlic or whatever other flavours take your fancy.

200g (7oz) cashew nuts
finely grated zest and juice of 1 lemon
1 spring onion (white part only)
1–2 Medjool dates, pitted
2 teaspoons walnut oil or grapeseed oil
salt and pepper

Soak the cashew nuts for about 8 hours, or overnight, until softened. This will make them easier to blend to a creamy consistency.
Drain and rinse the cashews then add to a high-speed blender with the zest and juice of the lemon, the white part of the spring onion, dates, walnut or grapeseed oil and 200ml (7fl oz) water.
Blend on a high speed until the dressing is smooth and is similar in consistency to thick double cream. Season to taste and add more water if you prefer a thinner consistency.
Pour the mayo into a jar or sealable container until needed and place in the fridge to chill.

RED PEPPER HUMMUS

Serve as a salad dressing or as a raw dip – just make sure the hummus is of a pouring consistency if you want to use it as a dressing by thinning with a little extra water. Team it with the Green-on-Green Salad (see page 81) or Sweet Potato & Pea Salad (see page 73).

1 small courgette, trimmed
150g (5½oz) sprouted chickpeas or any sprouted seeds
1 garlic clove, peeled
2 teaspoons sesame seeds
finely grated zest and juice of 1 large lemon
salt and pepper

Peel the courgette and put it in a food processor with the rest of the ingredients and 100ml (3½fl oz) water. Blend until smooth, season, and thin with a little extra water, if needed.

BASIC PESTO

Pesto is like a stalwart friend when it comes to dressings. I like to thin it down with a little lemon juice, raw apple cider vinegar or other flavoursome dressing-compatible liquid, and hey 'pesto' I have an instant sauce to anoint a salad or steamed or roasted vegetables.

Pesto doesn't have to be the traditional basil, pine nut, garlic, Parmesan combo; you can sub the basil for other soft-leaf herbs or greens such as spinach, nettle tops, spring greens or kale. Likewise, pine nuts can be replaced with pistachios, Brazil nuts, almonds, roasted peanuts, walnuts or sunflower seeds. Or make a red pesto with tomatoes, roasted peppers and chillies. Ditch the cheese or use a different variety, such as goats' cheese, feta or... the options are almost endless!

3 tablespoons pine nuts, almonds, pistachios, cashew nuts or pumpkin seeds, or nut or seed of choice
1 peeled garlic clove, or 1 peeled shallot, or 1 trimmed spring onion
1 small handful of basil leaves, coriander, mint, tarragon, parsley, rocket, cavolo nero (dino kale) or herb of choice
2 tablespoons Parmesan, grated
1 teaspoon lemon juice
(to keep the pesto green)
4 tablespoons cold-pressed extra virgin olive oil, plus extra to cover
salt

Blitz the nuts or seeds and garlic in a food processor. Add the basil, or green or herb of choice, and Parmesan cheese and pulse again.
Pour in the lemon juice and olive oil and pulse again until combined to a coarse sauce-like consistency. Season with salt to taste.
Spoon the pesto into an airtight lidded jar, pour over enough oil to cover, and store in the fridge for up to 1 week.

SPRING CABBAGE & KALE PESTO

This super-greens pesto works equally as well without the Parmesan. Substitute almonds, macadamia nuts or hazelnuts for the peanuts, and try it spooned over the Avocado 'Truffle' Salad (see page 27), Summer Squash Salad (see page 37), or the Crunchy Winter Veg Salad (see page 75).

1 handful of spring cabbage or collard greens
1 small bunch of cavolo nero (dino kale)
3 garlic cloves, peeled
30g (1oz) Parmesan, grated
3 tablespoons cold-pressed extra virgin olive oil,
plus extra to cover
40g (1½oz) unsalted roasted peanuts
finely grated zest and juice of 1 lemon
salt and pepper

Tear or cut the leaves away from the tough stems of the spring cabbage and cavolo nero (dino kale). Blanch the greens in boiling salted water for about 1 minute until softened in texture and flavour, then drain well and pat dry with kitchen paper.

Coarsely chop the greens (you can juice the stems) and add to a food processor with the other ingredients then process until finely chopped to the consistency you desire. Season and process briefly again.

Spoon the pesto into an airtight lidded jar, pour over enough oil to cover, and store in the fridge for up to 1 week.

LEMONY SALSA VERDE

Bright, fresh and bracing, this dressing is great with the Radish, Beetroot & Orange Salad (see page 35) and the Avocado, Tomato & Lettuce Salad (see page 38), or served poured over grilled chicken or fish.

finely grated zest and juice of 1 lemon
1 shallot, peeled
1 garlic clove, peeled
1 handful of mixed herbs, such as parsley, chives,
coriander, mint and dill
100ml (3½fl oz) cold-pressed extra virgin olive oil
salt and pepper

Add the lemon zest and juice to a food processor with the shallot, garlic and herbs. Process briefly until roughly chopped, then gradually add the olive oil through the funnel, with the motor still running, until you have a fairly smooth dressing. Season to taste.

GREMOLATA-STYLE DRESSING

Gremolata is a popular Italian herb and lemon condiment, and in this recipe the essence of the accompaniment is turned into a fresh and zesty dressing that goes well with the Summer Squash Salad (see page 37).

finely grated zest and juice of 1 lemon and 1 lime
2–3 tablespoons cold-pressed extra virgin olive oil
1 handful of chopped mixed herbs, such as dill,
mint, basil and chives
1–2 teaspoons date paste or sweetener of choice
1 small green chilli, deseeded (optional)
salt and pepper

Blend together all the ingredients in a high-speed blender or food processor, or whisk together by hand until smooth. Season to taste.

TOMATO DRESSING

Delicious with the Swiss Chard & Tomato Salad (see page 83), this dressing also works well as a raw pasta sauce with vegetable 'noodles' as well as a type of raw ketchup.

If you're keeping the dressing completely raw, use the date paste as a sweetener and omit the mustard.

300g (10½oz) cherry tomatoes
1 large red pepper
2 shallots, peeled
1 large garlic clove, peeled
1 handful of mixed herbs, such as basil, parsley and
oregano
1 teaspoon date paste or maple syrup
1 teaspoon wholegrain mustard
finely grated zest and juice of 1 lemon
salt and pepper

Deseed and roughly chop the tomatoes and pepper. Blitz all the dressing ingredients together in a food processor until liquefied, but still slightly chunky. Season to taste.

ASIAN-INSPIRED DRESSING

The miso paste enhances the richness of this sweet, sour and spicy dressing. It goes well with any vegetable 'noodle' dish – try it instead of the Coconut Curry Sauce on the Veggie 'Noodles' (see page 93), with the Beetroot Carpaccio (see page 47) or the Mango, Beetroot, Kale & Radish Salad (see page 109).

1cm ($\frac{1}{2}$in) piece fresh root ginger, peeled
1 garlic clove, peeled
2 tablespoons sesame oil
finely grated zest and juice of 1 lime
2 Medjool dates, pitted
2 tablespoons miso paste
2 tablespoons soy sauce

Grate the ginger and garlic. Blend all the ingredients together with 2 tablespoons water in a high-speed blender or food processor until combined.

PEANUT SATAY DRESSING

Ready-made peanut butter is a nifty shortcut to a quick dressing, but you can of course make your own by blending blanched or roasted peanuts with a tiny bit of oil in a high-speed blender. This works well with the simple Carrot 'Noodle' Salad (see page 89).

3 tablespoons organic peanut butter or tahini
3 tablespoons orange juice
salt and pepper

Whisk together all the dressing ingredients with 1 tablespoon water in a bowl. Season to taste.

GINGER & WASABI DRESSING

This dressing lends a fiery kick to simple salads such as the Rainbow Chard & Black Radish Salad (see page 61).

2.5cm (1in) piece fresh root ginger, peeled
1 tablespoon lime juice
2 tablespoons cold-pressed extra virgin olive oil
1–2 teaspoons wasabi paste

Grate the ginger and mix together with the rest of ingredients, adjusting the quantity of wasabi to suit your taste.

MOROCCAN DRESSING

This aromatic dressing features the beautiful Moroccan spice blend ras-el-hanout, which is usually made up of at least 20 different ingredients. The blend I use includes galangal, black pepper, ginger, cardamom, cayenne, allspice, nigella, cinnamon, cassia, coriander, nutmeg, cloves, mace, lavender and dried rose buds and has a wonderful fragrant, warming flavour. Serve the dressing with the Middle Eastern-inspired Summer Salad (see page 51).

1$\frac{1}{2}$ teaspoons ras-el-hanout, plus extra to serve
3 tablespoons walnut or pistachio oil
juice of 1 lemon
1–2 teaspoons date paste or sweetener of choice
1 small red chilli, deseeded (optional)
salt and pepper

Blend together all the ingredients in a high-speed blender or food processor, or whisk them by hand. If you trickle the oil in slowly as you blend, it will help the dressing to emulsify and thicken.
Season to taste, then cover and store in the fridge until needed (it will happily keep for up to 1 week). Serve garnished with a whole star anise, if you wish.

ZA'ATAR DRESSING

Za'atar is a Middle Eastern blend of thyme, oregano, sumac and sesame seeds and gives a lovely zingy flavour to a salad dressing. Here, the spice and herb mix is teamed up with chilli, lemon juice and sesame oil to make a dressing that goes well with the Smashed Cucumber Salad (see page 74).

2 tablespoons sesame oil
2 teaspoons lemon juice
1–2 teaspoons za'atar
1–2 red chillies, deseeded, depending on how hot
the chillies are or how spicy you like your dressing
salt and pepper

To make the dressing, whisk together the sesame oil, lemon juice and za'atar. Finely chop the red chillies and stir them in. Season to taste.

CREAMY TURMERIC DRESSING

This creamy yellow dressing adds a bolt of colour to a salad as well as anti-inflammatory and other amazing medicinal benefits, thanks to the fresh turmeric. It looks and tastes great with the Courgette & Candy Beetroot Salad (see page 69).

100g (3½oz) cashew nuts
2.5cm (1in) piece fresh turmeric or 2 teaspoons ground turmeric
1 tablespoon raw apple cider vinegar
salt and pepper

Blend the cashew nuts with the other dressing ingredients and 100ml (3½fl oz) water in a high-speed blender until smooth and creamy. (If your blender isn't powerful enough to blitz everything to a smooth consistency, either juice the turmeric first (or use 2 teaspoons ground turmeric) and soak the cashew nuts for about 8 hours, or overnight, before blending.)

ACAI BERRY DRESSING

The acai berry is a wonder food in terms of nutritional value and makes a great dressing with its naturally sweet-sour taste. It is often sold in powdered form so is easy to incorporate into smoothies and dressings, and its stunning dark purple colour complements the Red Cabbage & Courgette Ruffle Salad (see page 33) perfectly.

2 teaspoons acai berry powder
3 tablespoons apple juice
1 teaspoon pomegranate molasses

To make the dressing, blend the ingredients together until smooth.

SPIRULINA DRESSING

Spirulina is a type of blue-green algae super-food. I've used the powdered version here. It has quite an acquired taste so up the sweetener if the dressing tastes too bitter for you. I serve it with the Rocket & Radish Salad (see page 97) or drizzled over fresh fruit salad.

½ teaspoon spirulina powder
finely grated zest and juice of 1 lemon
2 teaspoons date paste or sweetener of choice

Blend together all the ingredients until smooth.

RAW 'CHOCOLATE' SAUCE

Raw cacao is a delicious super-food, full of antioxidants, vitamins and minerals. This recipe makes a rich, glossy sauce, which is a great alternative to the white chocolate sauce for the Snowberry Salad (see page 115), or simply pour it over raw banana ice cream.

4 tablespoons coconut oil
1 vanilla pod
3 tablespoons raw cacao powder
2 tablespoons raw honey or sweetener of choice

Gently melt the coconut oil and scrape the seeds from the vanilla pod. Place all the ingredients in a high-speed blender and process to a silky dark chocolate sauce.

SPICED YOGURT DRIZZLE

Yogurt makes a wonderful dip, drizzle or dressing for any sweet or savoury dish, but if you're dairy free then try a nut-based or coconut yogurt alternative. Try this spiced yogurt with chopped fresh fruit, as a dip for sweet crudités or poured over the Red Fruit Salad (see page 111) or Dragon Fruit Salad (see page 99), with or without the passion fruit and clementine dressing.

200ml (7fl oz) natural yogurt (or a raw version made with 100g/3½oz cashew nuts, 100ml/3½fl oz coconut water and 2 pitted Medjool dates blended to a smooth consistency)
finely grated zest and juice of 1 orange
2 teaspoons maple syrup or sweetener of choice
½ teaspoon berbere spice mix, sumac or ground cinnamon

Whisk or blend together all the ingredients until combined. Serve sprinkled with orange zest and sumac and garnished with a cinnamon stick, if you wish.

Left-right: Creamy Turmeric Dressing, Spiced Yogurt Drizzle, Spirulina Dressing, Za'atar Dressing, Moroccan Dressing.

toppings

There are almost endless aesthetic, flavoursome and nutritious things you can top or sprinkle over your salad to add a final flourish, a bit of pizzazz, a flavour explosion and hopefully that 'wow' factor that will get people coming back for second helpings.

Why add toppings and sprinkles...

❋ to add that 'X-factor' to your salads

❋ as a final layer of flavour and colour

❋ to add a protein element, including nuts and seeds, tofu, flaked cooked fish, chargrilled chicken or barbecued meats

❋ to add an extra textural element – placed on top, rather than mixed in, will ensure your topping stays crispy and crunchier for longer.

PIMP YOUR SALAD!

I always love to add a few finishing touches to my salads and it can be as simple as a handful of fresh-from-the-garden herbs or sparkling, jewel-like pomegranate seeds to more elaborate flavour-packed vegetable powders, or a palate-teasing umami sprinkle. All of these, and my ideas below, will add another element of visual interest, flavour and texture to your salads.

The following are just some of my favourite things I use to pimp my salads (bear in mind that toppings or sprinkles are best added at the last minute, so they don't become soggy or even get lost in a salad):

❋ Edible fresh flowers, including floral, herb and vegetable flowers. Szechuan buttons (little yellow flower buds) are worth hunting out and give a tingling sensation when you eat them.

❋ Baby salad leaves, pea shoots, micro-greens, micro-herbs or pale green celery leaves.

❋ Baby vegetables, including carrots or courgettes, or vegetable or herb seedlings, or thinly shaved vegetables slices.

❋ Microplane-grated nuts, such as almonds and macadamia, for a pretty Parmesan-like topping.

❋ Nuts and seeds (whole or chopped), plain, toasted or sweet-spiced, or savoury granola.

❋ Attractively or artfully cut fruits and vegetables.

❋ Wild and foraged blackberries, elderflowers, wild garlic leaves or flowers, or dandelion leaves.

❋ Fronds of decorative herbs, such as dill or bronze fennel.

❋ Colourful dried fruit.

❋ Croutons (toasted, baked or fried) made from sourdough, rye, polenta, potatoes or sweet potatoes.

❋ Colourful fruit, vegetable and super-food powders, including blueberry, citrus, tomato, herb, acai berry, spirulina or chlorella.

❋ Seaweed, or other edible sea vegetables, such as nori sheets, kombu or seaweed 'confetti'.

❋ Sprouted seeds and beans.

❋ Cooked vegetables, such as caramelized roasted veg.

❋ Pickles and fermented vegetables, such as olives, capers, caperberries or kimchi.

❋ Coconut shavings, bee pollen, chai seeds or toasted buckwheat.

❋ Vegetable crisps, dehydrated fruits and vegetables or crispy fried herbs.

❋ Edible glitter or edible gold leaf or powder – for special occasions!

SPICED POTATO CROUTONS

You can make these with sweet potatoes or white potatoes, but the latter will take slightly longer to cook.

4–5 large potatoes, scrubbed
3 tablespoons cold-pressed extra virgin olive oil or melted coconut oil
2 teaspoons dried or chopped fresh herbs
1 teaspoon ras-el-hanout
2 garlic cloves, peeled and finely chopped
salt and pepper

Preheat the oven to 220°C (425°F) Gas Mark 7 and warm 2–3 roasting trays.

Cut the potatoes into 5mm (¼in) dice and put them in a bowl with the oil, herbs, spice, garlic and some seasoning then turn until evenly coated. Tip them on to the warmed roasting trays and spread out into a single, even layer.

Roast the potatoes for 20–30 minutes or until cooked through, golden brown and crispy. Transfer to a kitchen paper-lined dish until ready to serve.

PARMESAN CRISPS

Simple to make and delicious, these are a great way to get a non-salad lover to take a second look, or bite.

100g (3½oz) Parmesan, finely grated

Preheat the oven to 180°C (350°F) Gas Mark 4 and line a baking tray with greaseproof paper.

Place tablespoons of the grated Parmesan, leaving space between each mound, on the lined baking tray. Flatten each mound slightly with your finger then cook in the oven for 5–10 minutes until golden brown and bubbling.

Leave to cool slightly, then transfer to a wire rack with a spatula and allow to cool completely before using.

FRIED SAGE LEAVES

Often served as part of an apéritif in Italy, these also make a great crispy topping for a salad – even if you're not a big lover of sage, the leaves seem to mellow in flavour when cooked this way.

2 tablespoons sunflower oil
1 handful of sage leaves
¼ teaspoon sea salt

Heat the oil in a shallow frying pan over a medium heat and fry the sage leaves until bright green and crisp.

Remove, drain on kitchen paper and sprinkle with salt before serving.

MARINATED MUSHROOMS

The flavour of the mushrooms gets better the longer you leave them to marinate.

450g (1lb) mushrooms (white are fine but other varieties such as shitake, shimeji, enoki, crimini and oyster mushrooms are more flavourful), trimmed
4 tablespoons cold-pressed extra virgin olive oil
2 tablespoons white wine vinegar
2–3 garlic cloves, peeled and thinly sliced
juice of 1 lemon
a pinch of sugar (optional)
1 small handful of mixed herbs, such as tarragon, oregano, parsley and thyme
salt and pepper

Tear the mushrooms into pieces, or cut any extra-large ones into bite-sized chunks, and place in a bowl.

Whisk all the other ingredients together to make a marinade and pour it over the mushrooms. Season, stir until the mushrooms are coated in the marinade, then cover and leave to marinate for 20 minutes or, better still, place in the fridge overnight.

Serve the mushrooms at room temperature.

CHINESE SEAWEED KALE

Essentially the same as kale chips, but by finely shredding the kale it becomes just like the crispy seaweed you get in Chinese restaurants.

1 large bunch of kale
2 teaspoons cold-pressed extra virgin olive oil
½ teaspoon sea salt

Preheat the oven to 150°C (300°F) Gas Mark 2 and line 2 baking trays with parchment or baking paper.

Tear the kale leaves away from the tough stems (you can juice the stems). Finely chop the leaves and toss them in the olive oil and salt until evenly coated.

Spread the kale out on the lined baking trays and cook in the oven for 5–10 minutes, turning once, until deep green and crispy. Remove and leave to cool.

RAW 'PARMESAN'

A dairy-free alternative for a 'sprinkling' cheese. It has the fine graininess of grated Parmesan and a similar salty, savoury flavour.

100g (3½oz) walnuts or blanched almonds
1 small garlic clove, peeled
½ teaspoon sea salt

Put in a food processor and blitz to a fine grainy consistency.

COCONUT BACON

A nifty vegan way to replicate the savouriness of traditional bacon.

2 tablespoons liquid smoke (or use 1 tablespoon
smoked paprika mixed with 1 teaspoon water)
2 tablespoons soy sauce, tamari or nama shoyu
1 tablespoon maple syrup or sweetener of choice
200g (7oz) coconut flakes (the larger the
flakes the better)

Preheat the oven to 180°C (350°F) Gas Mark 4 and line 2 large roasting trays or baking sheets with parchment or non-stick baking paper.

In a medium-sized bowl, whisk together all the ingredients, except the coconut flakes, with 1 tablespoon water. Once combined, gently stir the coconut flakes into the liquid and turn gently until coated.

Remove the coconut flakes using a slotted spoon and spread them out in an even layer on the lined baking sheets. Bake for 2–5 minutes until crispy and browned, then transfer to a wire rack to cool. The coconut bacon will keep stored in an airtight container for up to 1 week.

DRIED APPLE RINGS

Dehydration is a great method of preserving fruits (and vegetables) and they make a nutritious addition to a salad.

4–5 eating apples, peeled if the skin is tough
2 tablespoons lemon juice

Preheat the oven to 65°C (150°F) Gas Mark ¼.
Core and slice the apples into 3mm (⅛in) thick rings and brush with the lemon juice to prevent them discolouring. Place directly on the wire racks in the oven, making sure the rings are spaced out, and cook for 6–12 hours until dry but still slightly pliable. Leave to cool. This works for most fruits, including mango, strawberries and kiwi.

SUPER-SEED & NUT SPRINKLE

This nutrient-rich blend of ground nuts and seeds is great to sprinkle over anything you fancy, not only salads.

2–3 tablespoons each of walnuts, almonds, pumpkin
seeds, sunflower seeds, sesame seeds, hemp seeds
and chia seeds

Tip the nuts and seeds into a food processor fitted with an 'S' blade and blitz to a coarse, grainy consistency. Alternatively, use a coffee grinder to make a finer mix. Store in an airtight container.

UMAMI SPRINKLE

In Japan, umami is classed as the fifth taste. It adds an amazing depth of flavour to savoury dishes and although there are lots of ready-made versions available, it's really fun to make your own 'magic' umami powder. Sprinkle directly on to your salads just before serving.

25g (1oz) dried shitake or dried porcini mushrooms
1 tablespoon ready-made tomato powder, or make
your own (see page 140)
1 tablespoon kelp powder or kombu
1 tablespoon bonito flakes (optional)
1 teaspoon sea salt
a pinch of garlic salt
a pinch of dried oregano
a pinch of dried chilli flakes
a few grinds of black pepper

Place all the ingredients in a food processor, blender or coffee grinder and blitz to a fine powder. Store in an airtight container for up to 2–3 months.

For a vegan alternative, leave out the bonito flakes and add more kelp powder.

NUT & SEED 'BRITTLE'

Adds flavour and crunch to sweet as well as savoury salads.

50g (1¾oz) pumpkin seeds
25g (1oz) sesame seeds
100g (3½oz) chopped hazelnuts
100g (3½oz) raw buckwheat
2 tablespoons raw honey
a pinch of dried chilli flakes

Preheat the oven to 150°C (300°F) Gas Mark 2 and line a baking tray with parchment or baking paper.

Mix together all the ingredients in a bowl with 1 tablespoon water. Spread out the mixture in an even layer on the lined baking sheet.

Bake for 20–30 minutes or until golden and crisp, then allow to cool before breaking into pieces. Scatter over a salad.

For an extra savoury version, add a small handful of nori flakes or shredded nori sheets.

For a sweeter version, combine the nuts and seeds with 50g (1¾oz) dried fruit, such as sultanas, cranberries or cherries, 1 tablespoon maple syrup or sweetener of choice, and 1 tablespoon melted coconut oil.

Left-right: dehydrated fruit, Parmesan crisps, bread croutons, kale chips, Coconut Bacon.

QUICK PICKLED VEG

Quick pickles are so easy to make and add great flavour and crunch to your salads.

2 tablespoons mirin or rice wine vinegar
3 tablespoons lime juice
3 tablespoons fish sauce
1 tablespoon granulated sugar
1 garlic clove, peeled and grated
2 teaspoons grated fresh root ginger
300g (10½oz) prepared and very finely sliced or grated crunchy veg, such as radishes, celery, fennel, mooli, carrots, cabbage or cucumber
pepper

To make the pickling liquor, whisk together the mirin or rice vinegar, lime juice, fish sauce, sugar, garlic and ginger in a large bowl until the sugar dissolves. Season with pepper.

Add the veg to the pickling liquor, stir to combine and leave to marinate for 10–30 minutes at room temperature.

Just before serving, lift the veg out of the pickling liquor and use as you desire. (The pickling liquor makes a great addition to a dressing.)

QUICK PICKLED SHALLOTS

If you dislike the acidity of raw shallots or onions in a salad then giving them a quick bath in a sweet vinegar marinade draws out any bitterness and leaves them with a milder oniony flavour.

2 tablespoons red wine vinegar
3 tablespoons cold-pressed extra virgin olive oil
1 teaspoon granulated sugar
1 large shallot or similar sized onion, peeled and thinly sliced
1 garlic clove, peeled and thinly sliced
salt and pepper

To make the pickling liquor, whisk together the vinegar, olive oil and sugar in a bowl until the sugar dissolves.

Add the shallot and garlic to the pickling liquor, stir to combine and leave to marinate for 30 minutes at room temperature.

Just before serving, lift out the shallot and garlic and use as you desire. (Save the pickling liquor to use for a dressing.)

QUICK PICKLED FRUIT

Fresh fruit is just as good pickled as the more usual vegetables. You can leave the skin on the apples, peaches and nectarines as they soften during the pickling process.

2 tablespoons red or white wine vinegar
1 teaspoon granulated sugar
2 handfuls of prepared and sliced fruit, such as peaches, apples, watermelon, nectarines or pineapple
1 shallot
salt and pepper

To make the pickling liquor, whisk together the vinegar, sugar and seasoning in a bowl until the sugar dissolves.

Add the fruit and shallot to the pickling liquor, stir to combine and leave to marinate for 20–30 minutes at room temperature.

Just before serving, lift out the fruit and shallot and use as you desire. (The pickling liquor makes a great addition to a dressing.)

PICKLED SPICED GRAPES

Grapes give little bursts of sweetness to a salad. These quick pickled ones are also gently spiced with a slight acidic kick from the vinegar, and add a completely different flavour dimension to a salad – they're also really good with cheese.

400ml (14fl oz) rice wine vinegar
2 tablespoons granulated sugar
2 star anise
½ teaspoon fennel seeds
1–2 teaspoons dried chilli flakes
1 teaspoon salt
3 tablespoons orange juice
2 handfuls of small seedless grapes

To make the pickling liquor, whisk together the vinegar, sugar, star anise, fennel seeds, chilli flakes, salt, orange juice and 5 tablespoons water in a bowl until the sugar dissolves.

Take the grapes off their stalks. Add them to the pickling liquid, stir until combined and leave to marinate at room temperature for 30 minutes, or in the fridge overnight.

Remove the grapes from the pickling liquid (keeping the liquid to make a dressing). The pickled grapes can be made a few days ahead of serving and stored in the fridge.

FRUIT, VEGETABLE & HERB POWDERS

These powders are easy to make and give salads a wonderful flavour boost when sprinkled over as a finishing touch. Use sparingly as they are super-concentrated.

Drying the prepared ingredients in a dehydrator is ideal but spreading them out on a wire rack or on a baking tray set in an oven preheated to 65°C (150°F) Gas Mark ¼, or as low as your oven will go, works well.

Grind dry and brittle ingredients in batches. The best tools for grinding are a spice mill, coffee mill or a high-speed blender.

Use the powders straightaway or store in an airtight jar to keep them completely dry for up to 6 months.

Don't reserve the powders for salads, you can also sprinkle them over, and into, smoothies, granola, soups, sauces, puddings and baked goods, such as cakes, biscuits and bread doughs, or over fish and meat dishes.

Here are five to try, but do experiment with other flavours:

BEETROOT POWDER

Very finely slice 4–6 raw scrubbed or peeled beetroots. Place in the oven for 3–4 hours, or until completely dry and brittle and then grind.

HERB POWDER

Spread 2 bunches of soft-leaf herbs, such as parsley, coriander, thyme, sage and dill, out on a wire rack or baking tray. Place in the oven for 90 minutes, or until completely dry and brittle and then grind.

FRUIT & VEG POWDER

Prepare the fruit and veg – core, stone, remove any tough skins as necessary – such as strawberries, raspberries, kiwi, citrus, rhubarb, apples or carrots. Cut the fruit or veg into thin slices, taking into consideration that wet ingredients will take longer to dry out. Place in the oven for 5–6 hours, or until completely dry and brittle and then grind.

TOMATO POWDER

Slice 500g (1lb 2 oz) tomatoes as thinly as you possibly can. Place in the oven for 5–6 hours, turning once, or until completely dry and brittle and then grind.

CITRUS PEEL POWDER

Cut the peel from 4–5 citrus fruits such as oranges, lemons and grapefruit. Place the peel in a saucepan, pour over enough cold water to cover then bring to the boil and cook for 1 minute. Drain, rinse well in cold water, drain again, then pat dry. Place in the oven for 18–24 hours until completely dry and brittle and then grind.

INDEX

ABOUT AMBER

Amber's love of fruit and vegetables started from a young age as her parents had a large vegetable garden, so there was always a bountiful supply of fresh fruit, vegetables, salad crops and herbs right on the doorstep.

She previously worked in corporate marketing, and also ran her own freelance marketing consultancy. She discovered the concept of raw food two years ago, decided to try it out as an experiment but was so blown away with how amazing it made her feel after just a few days that she carried on eating that way!

Amber now eats an 80–90 per cent raw diet for health and vitality, but still happily cooks other foods for the rest of her family and just tries to find enticing and inventive ways to encourage them to include more (raw) fruit and vegetables in their diets.

One of Amber's passions is salad-making. She also composes artful arrangements of fruit and vegetables, turning them into eye-catching patterns and designs, which she sells as limited edition prints.

ACKNOWLEDGEMENTS

Thanks firstly to my parents for all their love and amazing support. For growing things, sourcing, measuring up, painting background boards, dog-sitting when I'm busy etc. etc. ... the list is endless! I couldn't do any of this without you. Also for passing on your passions (and a little of your creative talents!) for food, cooking and art.

To my partner Mark and our beloved chocolate Labrador Max; your encouragement (and woofing!) spurs me on every day.

To 'Juice Queen' Kara Rosen who spotted me on Instagram and gave me my first commission – I will be forever grateful. To Calgary Avansino and Valentina Zelyaeva for introducing me to the concept of raw food and sparking a fascination that quite literally changed my life.

To Viv Irish and Joy Hales (editors at *Derbyshire Life* magazine) who gave me my first break in food writing. To Jamie O and Pete, big thanks for your interest in what I do and for introducing me to the wonderful world of Instagram and the candy beetroot!

To the fabulous team at Octopus: to Stephanie Jackson for your gorgeous joie de vivre, enthusiasm and faith in me; to Yasia Williams for your creative genius and sweet patience with my endless flow of photographs; to Polly Poulter for editing me so beautifully, and to Karen Baker and the PR team for all their energies and activities in promoting this book. Also to my lovely literary agent Jo Cavey for appearing in my life at just the right moment.

Finally to my 'family' on social media, Instagram and to all those who follow my work – without you this book wouldn't be here.